AF652418

Quiz on Olympics

Master Yourself with Quizes

- *Quiz on Animals*
- *Quiz on Birds*
- *Quiz on Environment*
- *Quiz on Famous People*
- *Quiz on Geography*
- *Quiz on General Knowledge*
- *Quiz on History*
- *Quiz on Literature*
- *Quiz on Mythology*
- *Quiz on Physics*
- *Quiz on Science*
- *Quiz on Shakespeare*
- *Quiz on Sports*

Quiz on Olympics

Vijayalakshmi Iyer

GNOSIS
Nurturing the Aspirations

Worldwide Circulation through Authorspress Global Network
First Published 2010
by
Gnosis
E-35/103, Jawahar Park
Laxmi Nagar, Delhi-110092
e-mail: authorspress@yahoo.com

Copyright © 2010 Gnosis
An Imprint of Authorspress

Quiz on Olympics
ISBN 978-81-89012-88-5

Printed in India at Tarun Offset, Delhi.

Preface

The Olympic Games are an international event of summer and winter sports, in which thousands of athletes compete in a wide variety of events. The Games are currently held every two years, with Summer and Winter Olympic Games alternating. Originally, the ancient Olympic Games were held in Olympia, Greece, from the 8th century BC to the 5th century AD. In the late 19th century, Baron Pierre de Coubertin was inspired by Olympic festivals to revive the Games. For this purpose, he founded the International Olympic Committee (IOC) in 1894, and two years later, the modern Olympic Games were established in Athens.

The evolution of the Olympic Movement during the 20th century forced the IOC to adapt the Games to the world's changing social circumstances. Some of these adjustments included the creation of the Winter Games for ice and snow sports, the Paralympic Games for athletes with physical disabilities, and the Youth Olympic Games for teenage athletes. The IOC also had to accommodate the Games to the varying economical, political, and technological realities of the 20th century. From 241 participants representing 14 nations in 1896, the Games have grown to 10,500 competitors from 204 countries at the 2008 Summer Olympics.

This book in the quiz series brings forth the reader an almost encyclopaedic amount of information on Olympics since its inception. The focus is not just on increasing the readers' knowledge about Olympics, but also on fostering and encouraging readers to try out new sports, by providing them insightful and exciting knowledge on the subject. It is hoped that the compendious and informative nature of the book finds favour with the readers.

Vijayalaksmi Iyer

Contents

1

Ancient Games

1. In which year were the first recorded Olympic Games held?

a) *666 BC* b) *776 BC*

c) *676 BC* d) *766 BC*

2. Who recorded tales about the early Olympics?

a) *Arrakhion* b) *Melankomas*

c) *Pausanias* d) *Pindar*

3. Who created the Olympic Games?

a) *The ancient Greeks*

b) *The Celts*

c) *The ancient Romans*

d) *The ancient Egyptians*

4. The Olympics were held in honour of which Greek god?

a) *Zeus* b) *Apollo*

c) *Ares* d) *Hera*

5. Olympia, the site of the Olympic Games, was also home to one of the seven wonders of the ancient world. Which wonder was it?

a) *The ivory, gold-adorned statue of Zeus*

b) *The Olympic Stadium*

c) *The Colossus of Rhodes*

d) *Temple of Artemis*

6. **What was the only event held at the first Olympics in 776 BC?**

a) *A running race* b) *A sausage-eating contest*

c) *Discus throw* d) *Wrestling*

7. **During ancient times, whenever the Olympic Games were to be held, warring states would call a truce during the duration of the contest. What is this truce called?**

a) *Diaulus* b) *Ekecheiria*

c) *Pankration* d) *Halteres*

8. **What was the only Olympics event until 724 BC?**

a) *Chariot race* b) *Discus throwing*

c) *Wrestling* d) *200 yard footrace*

9. **What did competitors of the Games wear?**

a) *Toga* b) *Nothing*

c) *Long robes which were hard to run in*

d) *Loincloth*

10. **What was awarded to Olympic champions during ancient times?**

a) *Silver medal* b) *Gold crown*

c) *Wreath of olives branches* d) *Gold medal*

11. **How long did athletes train?**

a) *1 year* b) *2 months*

c) *6 months* d) *10 months*

12. **Athletes sought to bring glory and honour not only to themselves but also to . . .**

a) *Their favourite god* b) *Their city-states*

c) *All of Greece* d) *Their king*

13. **To be eligible to compete in the games athletes had to ....**

a) *Train faithfully for ten months before the games, remain under the eyes of officials for a month, and take an oath that they had fulfilled the training requirements.*

b) *Train faithfully for ten months, sacrifice a ram to Zeus, and take an oath to bring honour to their city-state.*

c) *Win contests at smaller festivals.*

d) *Train faithfully for ten months, and fast for three days before the games.*

14. Initially, women weren't allowed to participate in the Games. However, they could win the Olympic prize. In what event was this possible?

a) *Chariot racing* b) *Stade race*

c) *Trumpeting* d) *Pankration*

15. What would happen to a married woman who tried to attend the ancient Olympic Games?

a) *She could be thrown off a cliff.*

b) *She would not be let in.*

c) *She would be shooed off.*

d) *She would be made to kneel at the entrance.*

16. Which of the following groups could neither watch nor participate in the Olympics?

a) *Married women* b) *Slaves*

c) *Foreigners* d) *All of the above*

17. Who was the only athlete to have won three events in four consecutive stagings of the Olympic Games?

a) *Nero of Rome* b) *Leonidas of Rhodes*

c) *Herodoros of Megara* d) *Milo of Kroton*

18. The earliest recorded Olympic footrace was one stade in length. Which modern race would be the nearest equivalent?

a) *200 metres* b) *1500 metres*

c) *5,000 metres* d) *10,000 metres*

19. What is the long-distance race, known as the marathon, named after?

a) *The swift-footed Greek god of messengers*

b) *The hometown of Dikon, the track superstar of his day*

c) *A town north of Athens where the Athenians defeated the invading Persians*

d) *A famous sprinter*

20. Who is the only emperor to have been declared Olympic champion?

a) *Nero* b) *Tiberius*

c) *Caligula* d) *Commodus*

21. The pentathlon, consisting of a run, standing long jump, discus throw, javelin throw and wrestling, was believed to have been invented by whom?

a) *Plato*

b) *Jason (of the Argonauts fame)*

c) *Herakles* d) *Perseus*

22. How long was the diaulos?

a) *500 yards* b) *200 yards*

c) *1,000 yards* d) *400 yards*

23. The pankration event, added to the Games in 648 BC, was a mixture of boxing and wrestling. Which Greek philosopher was champion in this event twice?

a) *Aristotle* b) *Socrates*

c) *Sophocles* d) *Plato*

24. When was wrestling first introduced to the Games?

a) *776 BC* b) *708 BC*

c) *792 BC* d) *620 BC*

25. In the early Olympic Games, only free male Greek citizens could compete. After Rome conquered Greece, the Romans participated as well. Which Roman emperor competed at Olympia in a ten-horse chariot race?

a) *Augustus* b) *Nero*

c) *Tiberius* d) *Vespasian*

26. In which year did Theodisius I issue the decree which prohibited the Olympic Games?

a) *AD 363* b) *AD 393*
c) *AD 332* d) *AD 407*

27. When was boxing first viewed in the stadium?

a) *688 BC* b) *659 BC*
c) *701 BC* d) *640 BC*

28. What is an Olympiad?

a) *An athlete competing in the Olympic games*
b) *An ancient Greek unit of time*
c) *A famous statue of the Greek hero Herakles that athletes rubbed for luck*
d) *A place where the Games are held*

29. What was the name of the horse track in Athens Olympics?

a) *Hippodrome* b) *Diaulos*
c) *Stade* d) *Penthalon*

30. Which of the following was not an Olympic event?

a) *Boy's boxing and wrestling*
b) *A foot race in which contestants wore armour*
c) *A mounted archery tournament*
d) *A chariot race*

31. Only men of pure ... descent were allowed to compete in the Games.

a) *Roman* b) *Greek*
c) *English* d) *German*

32. When was the last Olympics held before being discontinued after an unbroken run of 1,168 years?

a) *AD 250* b) *AD 289*
c) *AD 375* d) *AD 393*

33. In 776, running naked, who became the first record Olympic champion as he won a foot race approximately 200 yards long?

a) *Coroebus* b) *Nero*
c) *Theodosius* d) *Phevos*

34. Name the town where the ancient Games were held.

a) *Athens*　　b) *Sparta*

c) *Olympia*　　d) *Markopoulo*

35. Which emperor banned pagan religions in AD 381 until which time the Olympics were recorded?

a) *Nero*　　b) *Theodosius*

c) *Heroditus*　　d) *Spartacus*

2

Modern Games

1. **The first modern Olympic Games were held in ....**

   a) *Athens, Greece* b) *Salt Lake City, USA*
   c) *Paris, France* d) *Oslo, Norway*

2. **The modern Olympic Games first took place in the year ....**

   a) *1896* b) *1856*
   c) *1897* d) *1846*

3. **How many sports were included in the Athens Olympics of 1896?**

   a) *15* b) *12* c) *9* d) *10*

4. **How many athletes competed at the 1896 Athens Olympics?**

   a) *100* b) *245* c) *121* d) *115*

5. **The very first marathon race ever run in an athletic competition took place in these Games. From which country was the winner?**

   a) *Greece* b) *Great Britain*
   c) *USA* d) *France*

6. **The principal founder of the modern Olympic Games, which began in Athens in 1896, was a French aristocrat, Baron Pierre de Coubertin. One reason for his interest in the Olympics was that he hoped to counter the contemporary tendency toward....**

   a) *An unhealthy obsession with appearance*
   b) *Alcohol abuse among teenagers*
   c) *Declining athletic standards*
   d) *Commercialism in sports*

7. **Twenty-seven-year old James Connelly withdrew from Harvard University to compete in the Olympics in Athens in 1896, and went on to become the first victor in modern Olympic competition. What was his event?**

   a) *The 100-metre dash* b) *The triple jump*
   c) *The decathlon* d) *The marathon*

8. **Which of the following events was not a part of the first modern Olympic Games held in Greece?**

   a) *Pole Vault* b) *Sprint*
   c) *Badminton* d) *Shot Putt*

9. **The modern Olympic Games are based on ancient games held in....**

   a) *Mount Olympus* b) *Olympic Mountains*
   c) *Olympia, Greece* d) *Athens, Greece*

10. **Where were the Games of the second Olympics in 1900 held?**

    a) *Rome* b) *Paris*
    c) *Athens* d) *London*

11. **How many women competed in the 2nd Olympics in 1900?**

    a) *12* b) *19* c) *0* d) *3*

12. **The 1900 Games took place in Paris, which was also hosting the World Fair that year. Organisational confusion was severe and the facilities were makeshift. Proper hurdles were unavailable, for example, so the competitors had to improvise hurdles from available materials. What did they use?**

    a) *Sawn-off soccer goal posts* b) *Desks from a nearby school*
    c) *Broken telephone poles* d) *Road construction signs*

13. **From 1900 on, women competed in some Olympic events, but it wasn't until the 1928 Games in Amsterdam that women's track and field events were included. Several participants in the women's 800 metre event collapsed after the race. As a result, ...**

    a) *Women's events were cut back.*
    b) *Lighter garments were introduced.*
    c) *Athletes were required to sign waivers before competing.*
    d) *Emergency oxygen was made available at all events.*

14. What happened for the first time at the 1900 Olympics?

a) *Women were allowed to compete.*
b) *An athlete ran the first four-minute mile.*
c) *Officials first flew the Olympic Flag.*
d) *The marathon debuted as an event.*

15. How many nations competed in the second Olympic Games in 1900?

a) *16* b) *22* c) *18* d) *20*

16. Which one of the following sports was not added to the Olympic programme for the 1900 Games?

a) *Equestrian* b) *Boxing*
c) *Soccer* d) *Yachting*

17. In which event did Ray Ewry of the USA not win a gold medal in 1900?

a) *Standing high jump* b) *Standing triple jump*
c) *Standing long jump* d) *Pole vault*

18. Which of the following sports (not previously included in the Olympic programme) was added to the 1904 Games?

a) *Boxing* b) *Cricket*
c) *Polo* d) *Rugby*

19. Where were the 1992 Olympic Games held?

a) *Athens* b) *Seoul*
c) *London* d) *Barcelona*

20. At which of these venues was the Olympic flame used for the first time?

a) *Amsterdam 1928* b) *London 1908*
c) *Athens 1896* d) *Los Angeles 1932*

21. In which year were the Olympic Games first televised?

a) *1936* b) *1965*
c) *1952* d) *1921*

22. **In which year did the idea of the Olympic flame originate?**

a) *1928* b) *1926*
c) *1927* d) *1925*

23. **The first Olympic Games to be held in Asia took place in Tokyo in 1964. Japan spent billions of dollars to ensure that everything would go smoothly. The "yamashita", named after Japanese athlete Haruhiro Yamashita, was popularised at these Games. What is it?**

a) *A silk robe*
b) *A judo throw*
c) *A high-protein drink*
d) *A gymnastics manoeuvre*

24. **In which decade was judo made an Olympic sport?**

a) *1970s* b) *1960s*
c) *1980s* d) *1990s*

25. **Which country won the gold medal in women's basketball in Athens 2004 Olympic Games?**

a) *USA* b) *Australia*
c) *Brazil* d) *Yugoslavia*

26. **Which country hosted the Olympic Games 2000?**

a) *India* b) *USA*
c) *Australia* d) *China*

27. **Who won the men's high jump gold medal in Athens 2004 Olympic Games?**

a) *Matt Hemmingway* b) *Andriy Sokolowskiy*
c) *Jamie Nieto* d) *Stefan Holm*

28. **Since they began, how many times have the Summer Olympics been cancelled?**

a) *Never* b) *Once*
c) *Twice* d) *Three times*

29. The Sydney 2000 games used three native Australian animals as mascots: Syd the platypus, Millie the echidna and Olly the kookaburra. Where did Millie's name come from?

a) *Millicent Parker, an Australian pioneer*

b) *Milliepillie, an Australian native plant*

c) *Millennium* d) *Millipede*

30. What sport did Bonnie Blair compete in?

a) *Judo* b) *Speed skating*

c) *Figure skating* d) *Water polo*

31. How long did the St. Louis Olympics (1904) last?

a) *A fortnight* b) *Five days*

c) *A week* d) *10 days*

32. As part of their training regiment for the 1988 Olympics, South Korean judo team members regularly spent an hour of the night ....

a) *In a super-heated sauna* b) *Alone in a cemetery*

c) *In a Buddhist temple* d) *Standing on their heads*

33. Which country won the maximum number of medals in Athens 2004 Olympic Games?

a) *China* b) *Russia*

c) *Australia* d) *USA*

34. In which year did Nadia Elena Comaneci become the first ever gymnast to score a perfect 10?

a) *2000* b) *1996* c) *1976* d) *1984*

35. Who won the silver medal for men's double trap shooting event in Athens 2004 Olympic Games?

a) *Ahmed Almaktoum* b) *Rajyavardhan S. Rathore*

c) *Zheng Wang* d) *None of the above*

36. Identify this great Olympian who won four gold medals as a member of the 1936 USA track team.

a) *Edwin Moses* b) *Rafer Johnson*

c) *Jesse Owens* d) *Bruce Jenner*

37. Only five countries have been represented in every Summer Olympic Games. What countries are they?

a) *Australia, France, Great Britain, Greece and Switzerland*

b) *Australia, France, Great Britain, Greece and USA*

c) *France, Great Britain, Greece, USA and Germany*

d) *Australia, Great Britain, Greece, Italy and USA*

38. Where did the Olympics take place in 2004?

a) *Sydney, Australia*

b) *Athens, Greece*

c) *Johannesburg, South Africa*

d) *Salt Lake City, Utah*

39. The Olympics were marred by tragedy at which of these venues?

a) *Mexico City* b) *Montreal*

c) *Munich* d) *Moscow*

40. What was different about Abebe Bikila?

a) *He was blind.*

b) *He was bitten by a dog during the race.*

c) *He lost a leg.*

d) *He wore no shoes in his first of two marathons.*

41. Which sport made its Olympic debut at the 1996 Olympics in Atlanta?

a) *Ultimate frisbee* b) *Beach volleyball*

c) *Surfing* d) *Skateboarding*

42. What are the two middle distance Olympic track events?

a) *800 m and 1500 m* b) *1500 m and 1200 m*

c) *500 m and 1500 m* d) *1200 m and 800 m*

43. Who won the men's 100 m sprint at the Athens 2004 Olympic Games?

a) *Maurice Greene* b) *Michael Johnson*

c) *Justin Gatlin* d) *Asafa Powell*

44. Which of the following women events was introduced at the Sydney 2000 Olympic Games?

a) *Athletics* b) *Hockey*

c) *Weightlifting* d) *Gymnastics*

45. Which of the following sports made its debut at the Sydney 2000 Summer Olympics?

a) *In-line skating* b) *Trampoline tumbling*

c) *Bowling* d) *Rhythmic gymnastics*

46. At which Olympics were competitors were all together at the closing ceremony?

a) *Berlin 1936* b) *Melbourne 1956*

c) *London 1948* d) *Helsinki 1952*

47. What were the names of the two mascots for the 2004 Olympics in Athens?

a) *Two Greek bears named Kairos and Nikkos*

b) *Spiros and Ajax - two serpents from Greek mythology*

d) *Athena and Phevos - a brother and sister named after Greek gods*

d) *Rhodes and Crete - two sisters named after Greek islands*

48. Who won the women's 100 m sprint at the Athens 2004 Olympic Games?

a) *Ivet Lalova* b) *Yulia Nesterenko*

c) *Lauryn Williams* d) *Veronica Campbell*

49. Who holds the Olympics record for the 100 m free style swimming?

a) *Aleksandr Popov* b) *Pieter Van den Hoggenband*

c) *Matt Biondi* d) *Rowdy Gaines*

50. In the 1970s, 17-year-old Olga Korbut of Belarus and 14-year-old Nadia Comaneci of Romania captivated audiences with gymnastic feats, launching the era of "pixie" gymnasts. In later years, both of these highly-accomplished gymnasts ....

a) *Settled in North America* b) *Married ballet dancers*

c) *Became school teachers* d) *Suffered crippling arthritis*

51. **Who won the men's shot putt gold medal at the Athens 2004 Olympic Games?**

a) *Yuriy Bilonog* b) *Adam Nelson*
c) *Manuel Martinez* d) *John Godina*

52. **Which country won the maximum number of gold medals in the beach volleyball events at the Athens 2004 Olympic Games?**

a) *Australia* b) *Brazil*
c) *USA* d) *Germany*

53. **Who holds the record for winning the maximum number of Olympic gold medals in athletics?**

a) *Maurice Greene* b) *Michael Johnson*
c) *Carl Lewis* d) *Kip Kater*

54. **Which country holds the record for winning the maximum number of Olympic gold medals in hockey?**

a) *Australia* b) *India*
c) *Holland* d) *Pakistan*

55. **Who won the men's 110 m hurdles gold medal at the Athens 2004 Olympic Games?**

a) *Colin Jackson* b) *Anier Garcia*
c) *Xiang Liu* d) *Terrence Tramwell*

56. **Which track and field event is Justin Gatlin associated with?**

a) *400 metres* b) *200 metres*
c) *100 metres* d) *1500 metres*

57. **Who won the gold medal for men's 200 m freestyle swimming at the Athens 2004 Olympic Games?**

a) *Pieter Van den Hoggenband* b) *Michael Phelps*
c) *Ian Thorpe* d) *Sebastian Coe*

58. **Since 1994 the Winter and Summer Games have been every ....**

a) *Four years* b) *Five years*
c) *Year* d) *Two years*

59. **In which year were the first Winter Olympics held?**

a) *1900* b) *1924* c) *1995* d) *1890*

60. How many medals have the Australians won in the Summer Olympics since the beginning till the 2004 Games?

a) *249* b) *286*
c) *327* d) *398*

61. In the 1904 Olympics, unsurprisingly, since 85 per cent of the competitors were from the USA, that country won 81 of the 100 events contested. How many countries attended?

a) *13* b) *33*
c) *23* d) *43*

62. Where were the Games of the third Olympics in 1904 held?

a) *Atlanta* b) *London*
c) *Philadelphia* d) *St Louis*

63. In 1908, there were five divisions in boxing. Incredibly, Great Britain won fourteen of the fifteen medals awarded. Which country was the other medallist from?

a) *Germany* b) *USA*
c) *Australia* d) *Cuba*

64. The 1912 Olympic Games were held in Scandinavia, the first time in that part of the world. Which city was the host?

a) *Stockholm* b) *Oslo*
c) *Copenhagen* d) *Helsinki*

65. Jim Thorpe, a Native American athlete from USA won two gold medals in 1912, but these were stripped from him following the Games as he was considered to be a professional. In 1983, thirty years after his death, his medals were restored. But for what events did he receive the medals?

a) *Pentathlon and Decathlon*
b) *Decathlon and Marathon*
c) *Pentathlon and Marathon*
d) *10,000 metres and Decathlon*

66. Who had the honour of opening the 1928 Olympic Games in Amsterdam?

a) *HRH Prince Hendrik* b) *Baron Pierre de Coubertin*
c) *Queen Wilhelmina* d) *Princess Juliana*

67. **The star of the 1932 Games was Mildred Didriksen, who competed in three events, and won two gold and one silver. In which events did she win gold?**

a) *Javelin and high jump* b) *Javelin and 80 metre hurdles*

c) *Long jump and high jump* d)
100 metres and 80 metre hurdles

68. **In track and field events in 1956, which nation won the most gold medals?**

a) *Soviet Union* b) *Great-Britain*

c) *Australia* d) *USA*

69. **In which month did the Melbourne 1956 Olympic games begin?**

a) *November* b) *March*

c) *June* d) *August*

70. **In 1980, what was Scotsman Allan Well's winning time that he shared with the Cuban silver medalist, Silvio Leonard?**

a) *10.35* b) *10.05*

c) *10.25* d) *10.15*

71. **Which Canadian in 1984 won the bronze medal in the men's Olympic freestyle wrestling?**

a) *Chris Rinke* b) *Daniel Igali*

c) *Bob Molle* d) *Gene Kiniski*

72. **In men's cycling mountain bike cross country in 1996, what was the name of the title-defender?**

a) *Thomas Frischknecht* b) *Paolo Pezzo*

c) *Miguel Martinez* d) *Bart Brentjens*

73. **Who was the first runner in 2000 with the Olympic Flame on Australian soil?**

a) *Ernie Dingo* b) *Nova Perris Kneebone*

c) *Dawn Fraser* d) *Bob Hawke*

74. **Where were the 2004 Olympics held?**

a) *Atlanta, United States* b) *Torino, Italy*

c) *Athens, Greece* d) *Sydney, Australia*

75. In which city were the 1908 Olympic Games held?

a) *Paris* b) *London*
c) *Rome* d) *Stockholm*

76. Which country won the most medals in the 1912 Games?

a) *Finland* b) *USA*
c) *Sweden* d) *Great Britain*

77. At the 1912 Games, the longest ever Olympic Games cycling road race took place, over 320 km. How long did it take the winner, South African Rudolph Lewis, to complete?

a) *8 hours 53 minutes* b) *10 hours 42 minutes*
c) *9 hours 22 minutes* d) *9 hours 58 minutes*

78. The United States won the most gold medals with 22. Which country was second?

a) *Finland* b) *The Netherlands*
c) *Sweden* d) *Germany*

79. Which country won the 1932 hockey tournament, beating the USA 24-1 along the way?

a) *Germany* b) *Japan*
c) *India* d) *Great Britain*

80. In 1956, this Olympic legend, a discus thrower, won his first of 4 successive Olympic titles (same event) with a throw of 56.36 m. Who is he?

a) *Jay Silvester* b) *Alfred Oerter Jr*
c) *Bob Mathias* d) *Mac Wilkins*

81. How many Britons finished the marathon in 1980?

a) *1* b) *0* c) *2* d) *3*

82. Which country had the most wrestlers in the 1984 Olympics?

a) *USA* b) *Russia*
c) *Canada* d) *China*

83. In archery men's individual, name the winner of the gold at the Atlanta 1996 Olympics.

a) *Rodney White* b) *Matteo Bisiani*
c) *MagnusPettersson* d) *Justin Huish*

84. Who was the host broadcaster for the Sydney 2000 Olympic Games?

a) *ASBA* b) *ATN7*
c) *SOCOG* d) *SOBO*

85. What was the name of the young girl who starred in the Opening Ceremony of the Olympic Games held in Sydney in 2000?

a) *Vicki Jones* b) *Kate Starre*
c) *Alyson Wilson* d) *Nikki Webster*

86. What was the demonstration sport at the 2004 Olympics?

a) *Wheelchair racing* b) *Golf*
c) *Tug of war* d) *American football*

87. Which country boycotted the 2004 Olympics?

a) *Great Britain*
b) *No country boycotted the Olympics*
c) *Switzerland* d) *Kazakhstan*

88. What were the names of the official Athens 2004 mascots?

a) *The Greeks* b) *John and Susie*
c) *Phevos and Athena* d) *Atheno and Athena*

89. The first gold medal of the 2004 Olympic Games was in which sport?

a) *Fencing* b) *Swimming*
c) *Shooting* d) *Archery*

90. Which country won most medals at the 1908 Games?

a) *Great Britain* b) *France*
c) *USA* d) *Sweden*

91. Track and field events for women were first held at the 1928 Games. How many events did they compete in?

a) *5 z* b) *8* c) *10* d) *14*

92. Which country won the 1928 Olympic soccer tournament?

a) *Argentina* b) *Uruguay*
c) *Italy* d) *France*

93. Which country dominated the men's swimming events in 1932, winning five of the six gold medals awarded, plus four silvers and two bronzes?

a) *Japan* b) *Hungary*
c) *USA* d) *France*

94. How many athletic events were contested at the 1956 Summer Olympics?

a) *33 events, 24 for men and 9 for women*
b) *17 events, 12 for men and 5 for women*
c) *56 events, 32 for men and 24 for women*
d) *42 events, 28 for men and 14 for women*

95. After his defeat in 1948 and 1952 (three silver medals, always beaten by Zatopek) which man was eager to win gold in the marathon?

a) *Abebe Bikila* b) *Alain Mimoun*
c) *Ali Bordin* d) *Yuosef Maala*

96. Who won the title for men's shooting skeet in 1996?

a) *Miroslav Rzepkowski* b) *Lance Bade*
c) *Andrea Benelli* d) *Ennio Falco*

97. What was the venue for beach volleyball at the Sydney 2000 Olympics?

a) *Manly Beach* b) *Bondi Beach*
c) *Homebush Beach* d) *Cronulla Beach*

98. Which country's team won the softball gold medal for the third straight time in 2004?

a) *China* b) *Japan*
c) *Australia* d) *USA*

99. Which of the following countries failed to win any gold medals in their own Games?

a) *Mexico in 1968* b) *Finland in 1952*
c) *Greece in 1896* d) *Canada in 1976*

100. Prior to the 2004 Olympic games, it was speculated that American swimmer Michael Phelps would meet or exceed Mark Spitz's Olympic record of seven gold medals in the Olympics. How many medals did Michael Phelps win in swimming?

a) *Eight* b) *Seven*
c) *Six* d) *Nine*

101. At the 1908 marathon the now standard length of 42.195 km (26 miles 385 yards) was used. Who was the winner?

a) *Dorando Pietri (Italy)* b) *Joseph Forshaw (USA)*
c) *Charles Hefferon (South Africa)*
d) *John Hayes (USA)*

102. A member of which royal family won the men's 100 m freestyle swimming event in 1912?

a) *Hawaiian* b) *British*
c) *Russian* d) *Danish*

103. Johnny Weissmuller of USA, who later became a movie star, won which event in the 1928 Games?

a) *Long jump* b) *Welterweight boxing*
c) *Highboard diving*
d) *100 metres freestyle swimming*

104. How many nations won at least one medal in an athletic event at the 1956 games?

a) *38* b) *10* c) *19* d) *27*

105. How many gold medals were won by the host nation, Australia, at the Sydney 2000 Olympics?

a) *13* b) *18* c) *21* d) *16*

106. Who read the athlete's oath at the Sydney 2000 Olympics?

a) *Matt Shirvington* b) *Andrew Gaze*
c) *Rechelle Hawkes* d) *Cathy Freeman*

107. Who won the 1500 m swimming at the Sydney 2000 Olympics?

a) *Kieren Perkins* b) *Grant Hackett*
c) *Eric Vendt* d) *Hayley Lewis*

108. Ellen Preis won the gold medal for the women's individual foil fencing competition in 1932, and remarkably was still fencing at the 1956 Games, where she finished seventh. Which country was she from?

a) *Austria* b) *Sweden*
c) *Germany* d) *USA*

109. This 18-year-old girl from Sydney won the 100 m and 200 m sprint events and ran a great final leg in the 4 x 100-metre relay to claim her third gold medal in 1956. What is her name?

a) *Shirlley Strickland* b) *Betty Cuthbert*
c) *Dana Everage* d) *Shane Gould*

110. What happened for the first time at the 1956 Melbourne games?

a) *In the closing ceremony all athletes were represented, not just the flag bearers.*
b) *It was the first time there was a closing ceremony.*
c) *The closing ceremony was washed out.*
d) *In the closing ceremony athletes did not walk in team formation*

111. At which of these venues was the Olympic flame used for the first time?

a) *Amsterdam 1928* b) *London 1908*
c) *Athens 1896* d) *Los Angeles 1932*

112. How long did the St. Louis Olympics (1904) last?

a) *A fortnight* b) *Five days*
c) *A week* d) *10 days*

113. The Olympics were marred by tragedy at which of these venues?

a) *Mexico City* b) *Montreal*
c) *Munich* d) *Moscow*

114. In women's hockey in 1996 which country was the defending champion?

a) *Korea* b) *Australia*
c) *Netherlands* d) *Germany*

115. In men's handball they won in Atlanta and defended their title in Sydney. But which country is it?

a) *Sweden* b) *Croatia*
c) *Spain* d) *Russia*

116. As part of their training regiment for the 1988 Olympics, South Korean judo team members regularly spent an hour of the night ....

a) *In a super-heated sauna* b) *Alone in a cemetery*
c) *In a Buddhist temple* d) *Standing on their heads*

117. How many athletes participated in the first Olympics?

a) *3,000* b) *312*
c) *500* d) *200*

118. Which of the following women events was introduced in Sydney 2000 Olympic Games?

a) *Athletics* b) *Hockey*
c) *Weightlifting* d) *Gymnastics*

119. In badminton, can you name the winner in Atlanta in the women's tournament?

a) *Fei Ge* b) *Mia Audina*
c) *Soo-Hyun Bang* d) *Susi Susanti*

120. Men's hockey was a great tournament in Atlanta. But who won it?

a) *Germany* b) *Spain*
c) *Netherlands* d) *Australia*

3

History and Trivia

1. **Which were the first three events that the athletes competed in at the Ancient Olympic Games between 776 and 720 BC?**

    a) *100 yard, 200 yard and 400 yard foot race*
    b) *200 yard, 800 yard and 1600 yard foot race*
    c) *400 yard, 800 yard and a variable length foot race*
    d) *200 yard, 400 yard foot race and a variable length foot race*

2. **At which Modern Olympic Games did they first use electronic timing devices and a public address system?**

    a) *1928 in Amsterdam* b) *1908 in London*
    c) *1912 in Stockholm* d) *1896 in Athens*

3. **The first Olympic Games for which we still have written records were held in 776 BC. At this Olympic Games, a naked runner, Coroebus, won the sole event at the Olympics, the stade - a run of approximately 192 metres (210 yards). This made Coroebus the very first Olympic champion in history. What was Coroebus's main profession?**

    a) *Cook* b) *Shepherd*
    c) *Mailman* d) *Soldier*

4. **Which of these was not a foot race in the ancient Olympics?**

    a) *Diaulos* b) *Stade*
    c) *Dolichos* d) *Marathon*

5. **In the Greece of 700 B.C, the Greek people would measure time in Olympiads, which were intervals of four years. This is**

why the Olympics are held every four years. Of course, the Olympics were not the only set of games played in Greece at this time. Which of the following was not one of the other three games that were played?

a) *Isthmian* b) *Nemean*
c) *Peloponnesian* d) *Pythian*

6. Hammer throwing is a sport that dates back almost a thousand years, to the 11th century. In fact, it was one of the sports that was played in the early Scottish games that was also in the first few Olympics. Which of these other sports were played in the first Scottish games, as well as the early modern Olympic Games, but is not played in today's Olympics?

a) *Tug-of-war* b) *Sabre tossing*
c) *Shot-putt* d) *Cockfight*

7. In which Olympic Games did drug testing make its debut?

a) *1964, Tokyo* b) *1968, Mexico City*
c) *1972, Munich* d) *1976, Montreal*

8. In the early 1900s, there was lawn tennis. This extremely popular modern sport was in fact only a game to play in one's own back garden before Suzanne Langlen brought it into the fore. With her interesting gait, incredibly graceful movements, and astoundingly short skirts, she shocked and amazed the spectators at the 1920 Antwerp Olympics. What nationality was this famous player?

a) *Swiss* b) *French*
c) *Polish* d) *Hungarian*

9. Baron Pierre de Coubertin was the key person in getting the modern Olympic Games going, but what nationality was he?

a) *German* b) *Spanish*
c) *French* d) *Dutch*

10. A major Olympic upset of the 20th century was the boycotting of the Moscow Olympics by the USA, because Russia entered Afghanistan. Sixty countries followed the USA in the boycott,

but the United Kingdom and many other European countries chose to participate in the Games. Which other city did Moscow beat to hold the 1980 Olympic Games?

a) *New York* b) *Harare*

c) *Paris* d) *Los Angeles*

11. **In 1766, the site of the original Olympic Games was rediscovered in Olympia, Greece, and exactly 130 years later, one man took it upon himself to revive the Olympic Games. He was also extremely purist in his views, and wanted all professionals to be banned from the games. Which of these descriptions best fits de Coubertin's attitude of the games?**

a) *The wreath or death for the participants of the Olympics!*

b) *Playing for victory is the goal of all sport, and victory shall be achieved at all costs.*

c) *The Games are a show of strength and courage of those whose profession is excellence, and should not be blighted by the common man.*

d) *The most important thing in the Olympic games is not to win, but to take part.*

12. **Only two countries have participated in every modern Olympic Games Greece and ....**

a) *France* b) *USA*

c) *Australia* d) *Great Britain*

13. **Which Olympics saw the first opening ceremony?**

a) *Athens* b) *Stockholm*

c) *London* d) *Paris*

14. **In which cities were the modern Olympic Games due to be held during the 'war years', i.e., 1916, 1940, and 1944?**

a) *Helsinki, Berlin and London*

b) *Berlin, Paris and Tokyo*

c) *Berlin, Tokyo and Helsinki*

d) *Paris, Tokyo and Helsinki*

15. Approximately how many years after Theodosius I abolished the Olympic Games, because of their pagan influence in AD 393, did Pierre de Coubertin begin their revival?

a) *1,500* b) *1,000*
c) *2,000* d) *500*

16. The Pankration was an event introduced to the Ancient Olympic Games around 648 BC. It combined which of the following?

a) *Boxing and wrestling* b) *Running and jumping*
c) *Boxing and running* d) *Discus and boxing*

17. In which year was the modern Marathon 'standardised' to a length of 42,195 metres?

a) *1928* b) *1908* c) *1924* d) *1916*

18. Where is the headquarters of the International Olympic Committee, the IOC?

a) *Los Angeles* b) *Sydney*
c) *London* d) *Lausanne*

19. There are five coloured rings on the Olympic flag. Which one of these is not the colour of an Olympic Ring?

a) *Blue* b) *Brown*
c) *Yellow* d) *Green*

20. According to Aristotle, which athletes "are the best, because they are naturally endowed with both strength and speed"?

a) *Pentathletes* b) *Pankratiasts*
c) *Runners* d) *Wrestlers*

21. Many philosophers in ancient Greece spent a lot of time thinking about sport and its connotations. Which of the following lines can be attributed to the great Greek philosopher, Plato?

a) *Animals not only play, but just like men.*
b) *For me, sport is a religion with church, dogma, ritual.*
c) *Man does manifest his warrior ethic in the games of Olympia*
d) *A man should spend his whole life at play.*

22. Although the Olympic Games have many of this type of sport today, no games of this kind were played in ancient Greece. They were not held in high regard by the Greeks, and even though the Romans set aside specific areas for these kinds of games, they were not spectator sports. They would be played on the street, while chariot racing was held in large arenas. What kind of games/sports are we talking about?

a) *Swimming, seen as a waste of time by both of the ancient cultures.*

b) *Archery games, mounted archery or 'Odysseus-style' bow and arrow sports.*

c) *Ball games, which were often played with pig's bladders or, even earlier that that, skulls.*

d) *Foot races of any length - chariot races were seen as the only way to compete.*

23. In 1976, a young Romanian by the name of Nadia Comaneci arrived at the Montreal Olympics. What was so special about this young gymnast and her achievement at the 1976 Olympics?

a) *She was the first person to clear 20 feet in the pole vaulting, despite it not being her competition of choice.*

b) *She was the first person to get perfect 10s from all of the judges.*

c) *She fell and broke her arm on the parallel bars, but still managed to compete.*

d) *She was the youngest person from Eastern Europe to ever win a medal in the Olympic Games.*

24. Although archery has always been an Olympic event, the Japanese samurai had their own variations, such as mounted archery, which came about as early as the sixth century. What was the penalty for missing the target in these games of mounted archery?

a) *The lowering of ranks - if the target was missed, the person who missed it would have their rank lowered by one level for every target they missed.*

b) *Death- the warrior would be set up by his fellow samurai if he missed a target.*

c) *Excommunication - every target missed would result in one day of being ignored by the fellow warriors.*

d) *Enforced suicide - if the target was frequently missed, then suicide had to be carried out by the person who missed the target.*

25. Which Games were the first ones televised and were the first to use telex transmissions of the results?

a) *1936 - Berlin*
b) *1948 - London*
c) *1932 - Los Angeles*
d) *1952 - Helsinki*

26. When was the exact length of the marathon established?

a) *1924 - Paris*
b) *1896 - Athens*
c) *1908 - London*
d) *1912 - Stockholm*

27. In which three years of the Modern Olympic Games were there boycotts by various Olympic teams?

a) *1976, 1980 and 1984*
b) *1968, 1976 and 1980*
c) *1972, 1976 and 1984*
d) *1976, 1980 and 1988*

28. What was the great Sanctuary of Zeus, the setting for the Olympic Games, called by the Ancient Greeks?

a) *Alsos*
b) *Megaron*
c) *Tumulus*
d) *Altis*

29. Aside from chariot racing, which other equestrian event, introduced around 648 BC, was held in the Ancient Olympic Games?

a) *Jumping*
b) *Horse Racing*
c) *Dressage*
d) *Cross Country*

30. In 1932, the second of the Modern Olympic Games to be held in the USA were in Los Angeles, with which of the following not being introduced for the first time?

a) *Olympic village*
b) *Photo-finish cameras*
c) *Televising of the Games*
d) *Victory platforms*

31. In which city were the Olympics held when the official Olympic flag was first flown?

a) *Paris*
b) *Athens*
c) *Antwerp*
d) *Stockholm*

32. As the Irish have shown, the Greeks weren't the first people to use sport as a method of recreation. How is it known that the Ancient Egyptians and Assyrians also participated in modern day Olympic sports, as far back as 4000 BC?

a) *Tomb paintings in Egypt show running, rowing, and archery being played by the Ancient Egyptian people.*

b) *Hieroglyphics were found, recording the popularity and spread of boxing as a sport throughout the Nile Valley.*

c) *Wall etchings that were located in Luxor, Egypt, show the Assyrian people swimming a stroke with the Greeks later called 'the crawl'.*

d) *All of these three answers are correct. The Egyptians left a lot of evidence for their love of sports.*

33. The Olympics have been held in London twice, but when was the first time?

a) *1908* b) *1930*

c) *1948* d) *1956*

34. Many games, played in the Olympics and in many other sporting tournaments, have basis in real life. Javelin throwing, for example, is as the throwing of a spear. Pole vaulting, the leaping of a stream by using a big stick. One such sport is the 'harrijasotzaileak', a sporting event played in the Basque regions of Spain and France. What does this sporting event actually involve?

a) *Live pigeons are shot from a distance of 500 feet, as a testament to the masculinity of the shooter.*

b) *A boulder or stone, weighing 350 lb (159 kg), being lifted to chest height.*

c) *A ball-and-chain contraption is heaved by pulling movements over the head. It is similar to hammer throwing.*

d) *This is very similar to the aforementioned pole vaulting, but weights are also attached the vaulter.*

35. Where were the Olympics held when the Olympic Hymn was first performed?

a) *Paris* b) *London*

c) *St. Louis* d) *Athens*

36. In which year were Olympic medals restored to Native American, Jim Thorpe?

a) *1982* b) *2000*
c) *1990* d) *1980*

37. Which was put in place by the Greeks before and during all the Ancient Olympic festivals?

a) *A public holiday* b) *A ban on taxes*
c) *A ban on drinking* d) *A truce*

38. Who was the Greek god honoured by the Ancient Olympic Games?

a) *Pelops* b) *Heracles*
c) *Zeus* d) *Perseus*

39. In which of the following three years were the Olympic Games not held?

a) *1936, 1940 and 1944* b) *1912, 1936 and 1940*
c) *1916, 1940 and 1944* d) *1916, 1936 and 1940*

40. The founder of the modern Olympic Games, Pierre de Coubertin, in 1921 used a Latin phrase of his friend, Father Henri Didon, for the Olympic motto. What was that phrase, now an Olympic motto?

a) *Certius, Dutius, Fortius* b) *Citius, Altius, Fortius*
c) *Citius, Amitius, Dutius* d) *Altius, Certius, Velotius*

41. In which city did the Olympic flame first appear?

a) *Amsterdam* b) *Los Angeles*
c) *Paris* d) *Antwerp*

42. Victor Boin was the first athlete to take the Olympic oath (Antwerp 1920). What was he?

a) *Runner* b) *Fencer*
c) *Boxer* d) *Weightlifter*

43. As most people believe, the Olympics are one of the oldest organised games in the world, but they are far from the oldest.

The first recorded organised games were held in Ireland much earlier than the first Olympics, but when were they held, and what were the called?

a) *From 490 to 396 BC, the Sparta games (held by Princess Kyniska) were the earliest games.*

b) *A Maori version of the games, called the Rungan Arii, are the earliest known, stretching from 1100 BC until AD 13, when the Maoris left their Polynesians homes.*

c) *Between 300 BC and AD 120, the Boudican games were the oldest, and were held in honour of Boudicca's greatness.*

d) *The games were held from 1800 BC until around AD 1180, and they were called The Tailteann Games.*

44. In which year was the official Olympic Flag first used at the modern Olympic Games?

a) *1920 z* b) *1912*

c) *1916* d) *1900*

45. The Olympic flame was first lit during which year of the modern era?

a) *1924* b) *1928*

c) *1900* d) *1904*

46. All of the people that participated in the Games were male, as the Greeks were in fact rather uptight as far as women and their participation went. This meant that the majority of the games were played in the buff, but which of these words has a root that comes from the naked nature of the first Olympics?

a) *Athletics* b) *Gymnasium*

c) *Vertissement* d) *Olympiad*

47. When were women allowed to participate in modern Olympic Games?

a) *1900 - Paris* b) *1904 - St. Louis*

c) *1896 - Athens* d) *1908 - London*

48. Which was the first city to host the Summer Olympic Games in the southern hemisphere?

a) *Melbourne* b) *Johannesburg*

c) *Rio de Janeiro* d) *Durban*

49. Which Roman emperor abolished the Olympic Games?

a) *Romulus Augustulus* b) *Theodosius I*

c) *Vespasian* d) *Constantine I*

50. In which year of the Modern Olympics were the Winter Games added?

a) *1936* b) *1924*

c) *1916* d) *1920*

4

Olympic Facts

1. Who was the 'inventor' of the modern Olympic Games?

a) *Joseph Brookes*
b) *Baron Pierre de Coubertin*
c) *Henri Zapeas*
d) *Alexander the Great*

2. Which five events are a part of the Modern Pentathlon at the Olympics?

a) *Cross-country running, archery, horseback riding, swimming and javelin*
b) *Cross-country running, swimming, pistol shooting, fencing and horseback riding*
c) *Fencing, pistol shooting, horseback riding, archery and cross-country running*
d) *Long jump, high jump, 100 metre hurdles, 1500 metres and shot putt*

3. The Olympic relay torch was introduced from which Olympic?

a) *Germany*
b) *Japan*
c) *USA*
d) *Canada*

4. Which of the following sports has not been an event at the Summer Olympics?

a) *Croquet*
b) *Tug-of-war*
c) *Pigeon shooting*
d) *Roller hockey*

5. The Olympic motto, *Citius, Altius, Fortius,* was taken by Baron de Coubertin from a Latin phrase used by a priest named who?

a) *Henry Didon*
b) *Vincent de Paul*
c) *Ignatius of Loyola*
d) *Maximillian Kolbe*

6. **What does the Olympic motto 'Citius, Altius, Fortius' mean?**

   a) *Go Big Or Go Home* b) *Faster, Longer, Deeper*
   c) *Swifter, Further, Stronger* d) *Swifter, Higher, Stronger*

7. **How many different types of canoes are there for the canoeing event?**

   a) *12* b) *9* c) *2* d) *4*

8. **The Olympic flag was introduced in 1896. What do the five rings on the flag symbolise?**

   a) *The union of the five continents: America, Africa, Australia, Europe and Asia*
   b) *They denote athletics, tennis, hockey, equestrian and boxing*
   c) *Modern man's five central emotions: love, hate, sadness, envy and lust*
   d) *The planet's five elements: earth, wind, water, fire and ether*

9. **In which of the following years were both the Summer and Winter Olympics held in the same country?**

   a) *1944* b) *1980* c) *1952* d) *1936*

10. **In one Olympics Japan and Germany were not invited. Which one?**

    a) *1948 London* b) *1980 Moscow*
    c) *1976 Canada* d) *1900 France*

11. **Who designed the Olympic Flag?**

    a) *Jesse Owens* b) *Pierre de Coubertin*
    c) *Samaranch* d) *Jule Rime*

12. **Which sport is not included in the Olympic Games?**

    a) *Swimming* b) *Soccer*
    c) *Fishing* d) *Gymnastics*

13. **With which sport do you associate the name Natalie Ward?**

    a) *Softball* b) *Badminton*
    c) *Athletics* d) *Water Polo*

14. **How often were the ancient Olympic Games held?**

    a) *Once in four years* b) *Once in ten years*
    c) *Once in two years* d) *Once in five years*

15. In the Ancient Olympic Games which was the only ethnic race to enter competition?

a) *English* b) *Greeks*
c) *Palestinians* d) *Egyptians*

16. How many events are alike in the modern and ancient Olympic Games?

a) 2 b) 6 c) 5 d) 8

17. In which year was the Olympic Academy established?

a) *1961* b) *1971* c) *1981* d) *1951*

18. The Olympic torch burns all throughout the duration of the Games. Where is the Olympic torch lit?

a) *Temple of Zeus* b) *Temple of Hestia*
c) *Temple of Diana* d) *Temple of Hera*

19. What kind of people compete in the Paralympics?

a) *Rich* b) *Poor*
c) *Physically disabled* d) *Elderly*

20. From which country did curling come?

a) *Russia* b) *Germany*
c) *Scotland* d) *Ireland*

21. The International Olympic Committee (IOC) has been in charge of running the Olympic Games through its host member nations. All countries competing in the Games have to be a member of the IOC. Which country was the first to have two IOC presidents elected?

a) *France* b) *Belgium*
c) *USA* d) *Greece*

22. From which Olympics were the games of volleyball and judo introduced?

a) *London in 1948* b) *France in 1900*
c) *Germany in 1936* d) *Japan in 1964*

23. Of what nationality was the winner of the first modern Olympic marathon?

a) *Spanish* b) *Sweedish*
c) *English* d) *Greek*

24. How far is a modern day full marathon, in miles?

a) *28 miles* b) *24 miles*
c) *22 miles* d) *26 miles*

25. Mascots have become an accepted symbol for the Olympic Games, with each host country for both Summer and Winter Games coming up with their own. In what year and Games was the Olympic mascot officially recognised?

a) *1968 Mexico City* b) *1972 Munich*
c) *1968 Grenoble* d) *1972 Sapporo*

26. Which was the first year of equestrian in the Olympics?

a) *1912* b) *1916* c) *1992* d) *1948*

27. The Olympic Creed – "The most important thing in the Olympic Games is not to win but to take part, just as the most important thing in life is not the triumph, but the struggle. The essential thing is not to have conquered, but to have fought well." This was adopted by Baron de Coubertin after hearing it from a sermon by the Bishop of Philadelphia. In what year was the creed first used?

a) *1912 Stockholm* b) *1904 Paris*
c) *1908 London* d) *1900 St. Louis*

28. When and where was the first Paralympics held?

a) *Rome in 1960* b) *Atlanta in 1996*
c) *Barcelona in 1912* d) *Japan in 1964*

29. What is the slashing and thrusting weapon used in fencing?

a) *Epee* b) *Foil* c) *Sabre* d) *Sword*

30. What is the scale that synchronised swimmers are graded on?

a) *100-1,000* b) *0-10*
c) *1-10* d) *10-100*

31. How many people can be in the pool at once in water polo?

a) *6* b) *7* c) *8* d) *10*

32. Who composed the music for the Olympic anthem?

a) *Spyros Samaras* b) *Kostis Palamis*
c) *Grant Edwards* d) *Alaine Phevos*

33. During which Olympics had the International Basketball Federation proposed a rule (later withdrawn) that would have banned all players taller than six feet three inches?

a) *1936 Berlin* b) *1948 London*
c) *1952 Helsinki* d) *1956 Melbourne*

34. The two official languages of the International Olympic Committee are:

a) *English and Greek* b) *English and Russian*
c) *Greek and French* d) *English and French*

35. In London in ... the marathon was deliberately distanced to start at Windsor Castle so that the British royal children could view the start and finish in the stadium directly in front of the royal box of Queen Alexandra.

a) *1908* b) *1912* c) *1916* d) *1948*

36. The Marathon race commemorates a legendary feat from the year 490 BC. One of the Athenians brought the news of a battle victory from Marathon to Athens. After running all the way, what word did he utter?

a) *Eureka!* b) *Yabba-dabba-doo!*
c) *Hallelujah!* d) *Nenikekamen!*

37. In which year did India lose its winning streak in hockey after recording a feat of 30 wins?

a) *1960* b) *1964* c) *1968* d) *1972*

38. When was the first collective housing for athletes provided? The huts looked like army barracks!

a) *1900* b) *1912* c) *1924* d) *1936*

39. Which city saw the first specially designed Olympic village?

a) *Paris, 1924* b) *Amsterdam, 1928*
c) *Los Angeles, 1932* d) *Berlin, 1936*

40. **Who was the first athlete to fail an Olympic sex chromosome test, after winning a bronze in the 100-metre dash and gold as a member of the 4x100 metre relay team?**

a) *Eva Klobukowska* b) *Heidi Schuler*
c) *Taresa Edwards* d) *Rechelle Hawkes*

41. **Name the only Olympic competitor to win gold medals at six consecutive Games.**

a) *Mark Spitz* b) *Aladar Gerevich*
c) *Carl Lewis* d) *Matt Biondi*

42. **When were the first commemorative Olympic stamps released?**

a) *1896, Athens* b) *1900, Paris*
c) *1904, St. Louis* d) *1908, London*

43. **When were the gold, silver and bronze medals awarded for the first time for the first three places?**

a) *1904* b) *1928* c) *1936* d) *1948*

44. **Name the oldest competitor (aged sixty) to win an Olympic gold medal.**

a) *Victor Bion* b) *Georges Andre*
c) *Oscar Swahn* d) *Gary Denis*

45. **Olympia, the site of the Games, was also home to one of the seven wonders of the ancient world. Which wonder was it?**

a) *The ivory, gold-adorned statue of Zeus sculpted by the legendary Phidias*
b) *The Olympic Stadium* c) *The Colossus of Rhodes*
d) *The Temple of artemis*

46. **What distance is the Olympic marathon?**

a) *26 miles 385 yards* b) *26 miles 405 yards*
c) *26 miles 395 yards* d) *27 miles*

47. **The modern pentathlon includes fencing, cross-country running, riding, shooting and one other event. What is it?**

a) *100m sprint* b) *1500 metres*
c) *800 metres* d) *Swimming*

48. In rowing, the United States won the double sculls for the fifth consecutive Olympics. How many years before did they win this event again?

a) *44* b) *60* c) *36* d) *52*

49. The individual three-day event in equestrian was won for the second Games running by Charles F. Pahud de Mortages. Which country did he represent?

a) *France* b) *Netherlands*
c) *Great Britain* d) *USA*

50. Not surprisingly the USA won the most medals, including 47 per cent of the gold medals in 1932. Which country came second on the medal table?

a) *Finland* b) *France*
c) *Italy* d) *Sweden*

51. Where were the next Summer Olympic Games held after Melbourne?

a) *London* b) *Rome*
c) *Paris* d) *Tokyo*

52. On which date were these Olympic Games awarded to Athens?

a) *August 25, 1997* b) *September 15, 1997*
c) *August 5, 1997* d) *September 5, 1997*

53. Andrew Hoy, Rechelle Hawkes and Dawn Fraser have one thing in common. What is it?

a) *They are related to each other.*
b) *They are the only Australians to win three gold medals in the same event at three different Olympics.*
c) *They are all swimmers.*
d) *They are Australia's only ever Olympic medal winners.*

54. Which equestrian sport is trying to get into the Olympics?

a) *Combined driving* b) *Western pleasure*
c) *Vaulting* d) *Reining*

55. **Which of the following gymnasts is not matched with her best event?**

a) *Annia Hatch and the vault*

b) *Svetlana Khorkina and the uneven bars*

c) *Mohini Bhardwaj and the floor exercise*

d) *Carly Patterson and the balance beam*

1900 Olympics

56. **Which city hosted the 1900 Olympics?**

a) *Paris* b) *London*

c) *Melbourne* d) *Athens*

57. **How many nations participated in the 1900 Olympics?**

a) 25 b) 28 c) 24 d) 27

58. **The 1900 Olympic Games were held as part of the 1900 ....**

a) *World's Fair* b) *Sports' Year*

c) *Greek Year* d) *Turn of the century*

59. **Most of the winners in 1900 did not receive medals, but were given ....**

a) *Gifts* b) *Cups or trophies*

c) *Wreaths* d) *Ribbons*

60. **Some unusual events were contested in 1900 for the first and only time in the history of the Games - the equestrian high and long jumps, swimming obstacle race, ... and live pigeon shooting being foremost among them.**

a) *Tennis* b) *Badminton*

c) *Two-day cricket* d) *Basketball*

61. **In the coxed pairs and eights events in rowing, crews replaced adult coxswain with .... Their identities and ages were not recorded but they are believed to have been amongst the youngest of all Olympic competitors.**

a) *Women* b) *Children*

c) *Girls* d) *Greeks*

62. Three marathon runners from ... contested the result saying the French runners who got first and second places took a short cut, and the proof was they were the only contestants not spattered with mud.

a) *Britain* b) *France*
c) *Italy* d) *USA*

63. How many gold medals did the United States win in the 1900 Olympics?

a) *19* b) *16* c) *13* d) *10*

64. The ... tournament was notable as it marked the first appearance of women at Olympic level.

a) *Croquet* b) *Badminton*
c) *Tennis* d) *Swimming*

65. In cycling at the 1900 Summer Olympics which nation won five out of the six medals available?

a) *France* b) *USA*
c) *Germany* d) *Scotland*

66. Which sport made its debut at the 1900 Olympic Games with three events being held?

a) *Boxing* b) *Equestrian*
c) *Swimming* d) *Fencing*

67. The first football champions at the Olympics were the London amateurs of Upton Park F.C. A crowd of around 500 spectators saw them defeat their ... rivals.

a) *English* b) *American*
c) *Australian* d) *French*

68. Margaret Ives Abbott played in and won a nine hole golf tournament on an October Tuesday, 1900, in Paris. She died in 1955 without being aware that the tournament was part of the Olympic Games and she had become ... first ever female Olympic champion.

a) *Scotland's* b) *Italy's*
c) *America's* d) *Yugoslavia's*

69. **In which sport in 1900 Olympics did Mexico win its first ever medal in the history of Olympics?**

a) *Gymnastics* b) *Polo*
c) *Hockey* d) *Football*

70. **Rowing at the 1900 Summer Olympics competitions were held on which river?**

a) *River Rhine* b) *River Loire*
c) *River Oder* d) *River Seine*

71. **A combined Swedish/Danish team beat France for gold in the tug of war at the 1900 Summer Olympics.**

a) *Britain* b) *Australia*
c) *France* d) *Greece*

72. **How many gold medals did the host country get in the 1900 Paris Olympics?**

a) *20* b) *23* c) *26* d) *28*

73. **The first Olympic women's title was awarded to ... of Great Britain at Paris in 1900.**

a) *Eva Klobukowska* b) *Charlotte Cooper*
c) *Nadia Comaneci* d) *Taresa Edwards*

1904 Olympics

74. **The 1904 Olympics at St Louis was officially opened by ....**

a) *David Francis* b) *Theodore Roosevelt*
c) *Thomas Hicks* d) *William Garcia*

75. **How many women participated in the 1904 Olympics?**

a) *6* b) *9* c) *11* d) *12*

76. **Apart from boxing, dumbbells and freestyle wrestling, which other sport made its debut in the 1904 Olympics?**

a) *Badminton* b) *Tennis*
c) *Basketball* d) *Decathlon*

77. What game was featured as a demonstration sport in the 1904 Olympics?

a) *Tennis* b) *Basketball*
c) *Swimming* d) *Judo*

78. Which country won the most gold medals in the 1904 Games?

a) *France* b) *Australia*
c) *USA* d) *Russia*

1908 Olympics

79. In the 1908 Olympics, the ... team was expected to march under the Russian flag rather than its own flag, so chose to march without a flag at all.

a) *Polish* b) *Serbian*
c) *Finnish* d) *Romanian*

80. In the 1908 Olympics, the ... flag had not been displayed above the stadium, so the members of the team decided not to take part in the ceremony.

a) *Swedish* b) *Austrian*
c) *Dutch* d) *Italian*

81. The ... flag had also not been displayed above the stadium before the opening, so the flag bearer refused to dip the flag to the royal box.

a) *French* b) *Greek*
c) *American* d) *German*

82. In the 1908 British Olympics, the first runner to enter the stadium, Dorando Pietri of ..., collapsed several times and ran the wrong way. Not far from the finish-line, two of the officials took him by the arms, and brought him to the line. As a consequence, after crossing the line he was disqualified. Since he himself had not been responsible for his disqualification Queen Alexandra the next day awarded him a gold cup in recognition of his achievement.

a) *The Netherlands* b) *Poland*
c) *Spain* d) *Italy*

83. **For the first time the Olympic creed saying that "the most important thing in the Olympic Games is not to win but to take part" was publicly proclaimed at the 1908 Games, and its creator, a bishop from ..., uttered it at a mass held at St. Paul's Cathedral.**

a) *Germany* b) *Pennsylvania*
c) *Italy* d) *Britain*

84. **In the lightweight final of the 1908 Games in London, both fighters shared the same first name - ... - (Grace and Spiller) and both were from Great Britain. In the second round, each swung at the other and missed, and both fell flat on their faces!**

a) *Edward* b) *Michael*
c) *Frederick* d) *Allen*

85. **How many countries competed in the 1908 Olympics?**

a) *22* b) *44* c) *33* d) *11*

1912 Olympics

86. **For the first time, competitors in the Games came from all five continents, symbolised in the Olympic ..., at the 1912 Olympics.**

a) *Rings* b) *Games*
c) *Flag* d) *Stadium*

87. **Women's events in ... were introduced in the 1912 Games.**

a) *Basketball and softball* b) *Swimming and diving*
c) *Tennis and badminton* d) *Hockey and cricket*

88. **... took part in the first modern pentathlon competition in the 1912 Games.**

a) *King George V* b) *General George S. Patton*
c) *Prince Norodom* d) *Adolf Hitler*

89. **In athletics, ... were first used.**

a) *Whistles* b) *Batons*
c) *Spikes* d) *Electronic timing devices*

90. For the first time athletes from which nation took part in the 1912 Games?

a) *Yugoslavia*b) *China* c) *Serbia* d) *South Africa*

1920 Olympics

91. Where were the 1920 Summer Olympics held?

a) *Antwerp* b) *Paris*
c) *Sweden* d) *London*

92. Hungary, Germany, Austria, Bulgaria and ... were also banned from the 1920 Games.

a) *Italy* b) *Poland*
c) *Russia* d) *Turkey*

93. The 1920 Olympics were the first in which the Olympic Oath was uttered, the first in which ... were released to symbolise peace, and was the first time the Olympic Flag was flown.

a) *Balloons* b) *Kites*
c) *Doves* d) *Bubbles*

94. The 1920 Games also featured a week of winter sports, with figure skating and ... making their Olympic debut.

a) *Luge* b) *Skiing*
c) *Polo* d) *Ice hockey*

95. The Olympic motto 'Citius, Altius, Fortius' , meaning ... , was used for the first time in the 1924 Games.

a) *Faster, Higher, Stronger* b) *Higher, Longer, Stronger*
c) *Stronger, Faster, Longer* d) *Longer, Higher, Stronger*

96. ... was given formal recognition as an independent nation in the Olympic Movement in Paris in 1924 and it was at these games that it made its first appearance in an Olympic Games as an independent nation.

a) *Ireland* b) *Croatia*
c) *Nigeria* d) *Ecuador*

97. Ecuador, Haiti, Ireland, Lithuania, the Philippines and ... attended the 1024 Olympic Games for the first time.

a) *Finland* b) *Uruguay*
c) *Ethiopia* d) *Japan*

1928 OLYMPICS

98. Which city hosted the 1928 Olympics?

a) *Sweden* b) *Amsterdam*
c) *Antwerp* d) *London*

99. Who officially opened the 1928 Games?

a) *Prince Hendrik* b) *Prince Edward*
c) *Prince Norodom* d) *Prince Hirohito*

100. For the first time, in 1928, the parade of nations started with Greece, which holds the origins of the Olympics, and ended with the host country, a tradition which continues today.

a) *Australia* b) *Britain*
c) *USA* d) *Greece*

101. Women's athletics and which other debuted at these Olympic, in spite of criticism?

a) *Swimming* b) *Gymnastics*
c) *Tennis* d) *Marathon*

102. Which country took its first ever gold in field hockey in the 1928 Games, the beginning of a winning streak which continued until 1956 with six gold medals won during the period?

a) *Pakistan* b) *Germany*
c) *Holland* d) *India*

103. The 1928 Olympics saw the first appearance of the sponsor ... at the Games.

a) *Pepsi* b) *Adidas*
c) *Coca-Cola* d) *Nike*

104. Which country returned in 1928 after having been deliberately not invited in 1920 and 1924?

a) *Germany* b) *Switzerland*
c) *France* d) *Russia*

105. Which country won the 1928 Olympic hockey tournament?

a) *India* b) *Germany*
c) *Netherlands* d) *Great Britain*

106. Crown Prince Olaf, from which Scandinavian country, won a gold medal in yachting in 1928?

a) *Denmark* b) *Norway*
c) *Sweden* d) *Finland*

1932 Olympics

107. The first use of a ... was in the 1932 Games.

a) *Timer* b) *Victory podium*
c) *Flag* d) *Loudspeaker*

108. Tenth Street, a major thoroughfare in Los Angeles, was renamed Olympic ... in honour of the 1932 Games.

a) *Boulevard* b) *Avenue*
c) *Road* d) *Street*

109. What were the demonstration sports at the 1932 Games?

a) *Lacrosse and croquet* b) *Judo and karate*
c) *Basketball and softball*
d) *American football and lacrosse*

110. Colombia and which other country (with a single athlete) made their first appearance at the Olympic Games.

a) *Ethiopia* b) *Republic of China*
c) *Singapore* d) *Bulgaria*

1936 Olympics

111. How many nations participated in the Berlin Olympics?

a) *33* b) *39* c) *49* d) *53*

112. Film-maker Leni Riefenstahl, a favourite of Hitler, was commissioned by the International Olympic Committee to film the Games. The film, titled ..., originated many of the techniques now commonplace to the filming of sports.

a) *The Games*
b) *Olympia*
c) *Run and Win*
d) *Victory!*

113. By allowing only the ... to compete for Germany, Hitler further promoted his ideological belief of racial supremacy.

a) *Aryan race*
b) *Europeans*
c) *Men*
d) *Whites*

114. The Olympic Flame was used for the second time at these games, but they marked the first time it was brought to the Olympic Town by a torch relay, with the starting point in ..., Greece.

a) *Athens*
b) *Sparta*
c) *Olympia*
d) *Helos*

115. The Games were the first to have live television coverage. The German Post Office, using equipment from Telefunken and Fernseh, broadcast over seventy hours of coverage to special viewing rooms throughout Berlin and Potsdam and a few private TV sets, over Paul Nipkow TV Station.

a) *Ten*
b) *Fifty hours*
c) *Twenty*
d) *Seventy hours*

1948 Olympics

116. ... made their debut at the Olympics, both as outdoor sports.

a) *Badminton and tennis*
b) *Shooting and canoeing*
c) *Tennis and football*
d) *Basketball and handball*

117. ... *Three Principles of the People* was chosen the best national anthem of the games.

a) *The Republic of China's*
b) *The Netherlands*
c) *USA's*
d) *Australia's*

118. Basketball was added to the Olympic programme. In the final, the USA beat which country 19-8?

a) *Britain*
b) *Brazil*
c) *Canada*
d) *Spain*

119. **There was upset, too, in the team dressage in the 1948 Games. Which country left Britain with the gold medals but was disqualified a year later when the IOC discovered that one of its team member, Gehnäll Persson, wasn't an officer? The international equine federation at that time allowed only army officers to take part.**

a) *Sweden* b) *Norway*
c) *France* d) *Switzerland*

120. **The gymnastics intended for Wembley Stadium moved across London to the Empress Hall, Earls Court, to avoid the rain. Which country won the men's combined exercises and the individual pomelled horse?**

a) *Sweden* b) *Norway*
c) *Denmark* d) *Finland*

121. **For the first time, Olympic ... were awarded to the six highest placed athletes.**

a) *Certificates* b) *Points*
c) *Diplomas* d) *Ribbons*

122. **In the ... the starting block was first introduced.**

a) *Sprint athletics* b) *Marathon*
c) *100 m hurdles* d) *Long jump*

123. **Where were the opening and closing ceremonies held?**

a) *Empress Hall* b) *Arsenal Stadium*
c) *Windsor Great Park* d) *Empire Stadium*

1952 Olympics

124. **Who carried the Olympic torch at the Helsinki Games in 1952?**

a) *Paavo Nurmi and Hannes Kolehmainen*
b) *Heikki Savolainen* c) *Juho Kusti Paasikivi*
d) *Josy Barthel*

125. **Which country, with a mere 10 million inhabitants, won an astonishing 42 medals at these games, coming in third place behind the USA and the USSR with one of the most**

outstanding exhibitions ever?

a) *Hungary* b) *Portugal*
c) *Italy* d) *The Netherlands*

126. **Germany and Japan were invited again after being barred in 1948. After occupation and partition, three German states had been erected. Only West German athletes took part, from the Federal Republic of Germany and the Saarland which joined the FRG after 1955, the East German Democratic Republic being absent. Despite ranking 5th by total medals 24, Germans failed to score ... for the first and only time.**

a) *Bronze* b) *Silver*
c) *Gold* d) *Any medal*

1956 Olympics

127. **Which city hosted the 1956 Olympics?**

a) *London* b) *Helsinki*
c) *Tokyo* d) *Melbourne*

128. **The Games were officially opened by ... and King Gustav VI Adolf of Sweden with Queen Elizabeth II of Australia.**

a) *Philip, Duke of Edinburgh* b) *R.G. Menzies*
c) *H.E. Holt* d) *J. McEwen*

129. **... men dominated track and field. They not only won 15 of 24 events, they swept four of them and finished first and second in five others.**

a) *Germany's* b) *USA's*
c) *Russia's* d) *France's*

130. **Despite the international tensions of 1956 – or perhaps because of them – a young man from ... came up with a new idea for the closing ceremony. Instead of marching as teams behind their national flags, the athletes mingled with one another as they paraded into and around the arena for a final appearance before the spectators. That began an Olympic tradition that has been followed ever since.**

a) *Melbourne* b) *Sidney*

c) *Adelaide* d) *Perth*

131. The British and French involvement in the Suez Crisis led to the absence of Egypt, Lebanon and ....

a) *Jordon* b) *Iraq* c) *Iran* d) *Israel*

132. The Soviet handling of the Hungarian revolution led to the absence of Spain, the Netherlands and which other country?

a) *Germany* b) *Poland*
c) *Sweden* d) *Switzerland*

133. A third boycott came from the People's Republic of China, which protested against the presence of ....

a) *Vietnam* b) *Formosa*
c) *Hongkong* d) *Korea*

134. The Olympic Flame was relayed to Melbourne after being lit at ... on 2 November 1956.

a) *Sidney* b) *Adelaide*
c) *Olympia* d) *Athens*

135. The Olympic Flame was lit at the stadium by whom?

a) *Ron Clarke* b) *Con Verevis*
c) *Alderman W.J. Fulton* d) *Murray Rose*

136. Inspired by ... teenager John Wing, an Olympic tradition began when athletes of different nations are allowed to parade together at the closing ceremony, instead of with their national teams, as a symbol of world unity.

a) *American* b) *British*
c) *Canadian* d) *Australian*

137. Five nations competed in the equestrian events in Stockholm, but did not attend the Games in Melbourne: Cambodia, Egypt, Netherlands, Spain and ....

a) *Singapore* b) *India*
c) *China* d) *Switzerland*

138. Which country won the most number of gold medals in the 1956 Games?

a) *Russia* b) *US*
c) *Australia* d) *China*

139. Where were the rowing events held in the Melbourne Olympics in 1956?

a) *Lake Bonnie Doone* b) *Yarra River*
c) *Lake Wendouree* d) *Lake Eyre*

140. Where were the yachting events held in 1956?

a) *Port Phillip Bay* b) *Western Port Bay*
c) *Lake Wendouree* d) *Melbourne Bay*

1960 Olympics

141. In the 1960 Olympics, ... gymnasts won 15 of 16 possible medals in women's gymnastics

a) *German* b) *Soviet*
c) *Australian* d) *Chinese*

142. South Africa appeared in the Olympic arena for the last time under the apartheid regime. They would not be allowed to return until which year, after the abandonment of apartheid and during the transition to majority rule?

a) *1972* b) *1980* c) *1992* d) *1996*

143. Danish cyclist Knud Enemark collapsed during his race under the influence of amphetamines and later died in the hospital. It was the second time an athlete died in competition at the Olympics, after the death of Portuguese marathon runner Francisco Lazaro at the ... Summer Olympics.

a) *1912* b) *1900* c) *1920* d) *1932*

144. Which country broke India's dominance in Olympic men's field hockey by becoming the first team in history to beat India in Olympic field hockey since 1928 and winning its first ever Olympic gold medal in the process? India had already won 6 previous hockey golds in the Summer Olympics.

a) *Germany* b) *The Netherlands*
c) *Britain* d) *Pakistan*

145. In which stadium were the soccer/football finals played during the 1960 Games?

a) *Communal Stadium* b) *Flaminio Stadium*
c) *Olympic Stadium* d) *Adriatico Stadium*

1964 Olympics

146. Where were the 1964 Olympics held?

a) *Helsinki* b) *Sidney*
c) *Tokyo* d) *Paris*

147. The games were telecast to which country using Syncom 3, the first geostationary communication satellite? It was the first television programme to cross the Pacific Ocean.

a) *USA* b) *Germany*
c) *Britain* d) *Australia*

148. Who composed the theme song of the opening ceremony?

a) *Takashi Ono* b) *Osamu Watanabe*
c) *Yuji Koseki* d) *Yoshinori Sakai*

149. Name the person who lit the Olympic Flame. He was born in Hiroshima on August 6, 1945, the day the atomic bomb was dropped.

a) *Takashi Ono* b) *Osamu Watanabe*
c) *Yuji Koseki* d) *Yoshinori Sakai*

150. Name the two demonstration sports at the Tokyo Olympics.

a) *Baseball and judo* b) *Basketball and softball*
c) *Baseball and basketball* d) *Judo and softball*

151. How many nations made their first Olympic appearance in Tokyo?

a) *Ten* b) *Sixteen*
c) *Twelve* d) *Seventeen*

152. .... or Japan Martial Arts Hall, was built for the 1964 Olympics.

a) *Komazawa Olympic Park* b) *Nippon Budokan*
c) *Yoyogi Gymnasium* d) *Karuizawa*

1968 Olympics

153. How many nations participated in the Mexico City Olympics in 1968?

a) *82* b) *92* c) *102* d) *112*

154. In the 200 m medal award ceremony, two African-American athletes, Tommie Smith (gold) and John Carlos (bronze), raised their black-gloved fists as a symbol of Black Power. As punishment, the International Olympic Committee banned them from the Olympic Games for how long?

a) *For life* b) *One year*

c) *Three years* d) *Five years*

155. Which Mexican athlete became the first woman to light the Olympic cauldron with the Olympic flame?

a) *Vera Cáslavská*

b) *Debbie Meyer*

c) *Larissa Latynina*

d) *Norma Enriqueta Basilio*

156. Where were the gymnastics held?

a) *National Auditorium*

b) *Juan de la Barrera Olympic Gymnasium*

c) *Aztec Stadium*

d) *University City Olympic Stadium*

1972 Olympics

157. Which city hosted the 1972 Olympics?

a) *Paris* b) *Munich*

c) *Helsinki* d) *Seoul*

158. Who took the Olympic oath?

a) *Heinz Pollay* b) *Günther Zahn*

c) *Lasse Virén* d) *Heidi Schüller*

159. The Games were marred by what has come to be known as the Munich massacre. On 5 September a group of eight

Palestinian terrorists belonging to the Black September organisation broke into the Olympic Village and took eleven Israeli athletes hostage in their apartment, soon killing two of them; the subsequent standoff in the Olympic Village lasted for almost how many hours?

a) *18* b) *21* c) *20* d) *19*

160. Handball, which was last held in ... returned as Olympic sports after a long absence.

a) *1900* b) *1936* c) *1928* d) *1948*

161. Archery, which was last held in ... returned as Olympic sports after a long absence.

a) *1900* b) *1904* c) *1912* d) *1920*

162. For the first time, the Olympic Oath was taken by a representative of the ....

a) *Participants* b) *Referees*
c) *Judges* d) *Special invitees*

163. Which two sports were the demostration sports?

a) *Water polo and water skiing*
b) *Badminton and tennis*
c) *Water polo and badminton*
d) *Badminton and water skiing*

164. Name the mascot at the Munich Olympics.

a) *Misha, the bear* b) *Sam, the eagle*
c) *Waldi, the dachshund* d) *Amik, the beaver*

165. How many gold medals did the host nation, West Germany, win at the 1972 Olympics?

a) *13* b) *11* c) *15* d) *14*

166. Name the competitor who qualified for seven races and won all of them, setting world records in all of them, during the 1972 Munich Olympics.

a) *Carl Lewis* b) *Mark Spitz*
c) *Eddie Eagen* d) *Edwin Moses*

1976 OLYMPICS

167. Who took the Judge's Oath?

a) *Sandra Henderson* b) *Stéphane Préfontaine*
c) *Maurice Fauget* d) *Pierre St.-Jean*

168. It was the first and only time to date in Olympic history that ... of the Summer Games won no gold medals.

a) *France* b) *Greece*
c) *Australia* d) *The host country*

169. In protest at a tour of South Africa by the New Zealand All Blacks rugby union team early in the year, ... official Jean Claude Ganga led a boycott of 28 African nations as the IOC refused to bar the New Zealand team.

a) *Zaire's* b) *Congo's*
c) *Sudan's* d) *Nigeria's*

170. Which construction, a daring design of French architect Roger Taillibert, remains a lasting monument to the huge deficit, as it never had an effective retractable roof, and the tower was completed only after the Olympics?

a) *Maurice Richard Arena*
b) *Pierre Charbonneau Centre*
c) *Étienne Desmarteau Centre*
d) *Olympic Stadium*

171. The Olympic Flame was 'electronically' transmitted via satellite from Athens to which place by means of an electronic pulse derived from the actual burning flame? From there, it was carried by hand to Montreal.

a) *Ottawa* b) *Ontario*
c) *Quebec* d) *Manitoba*

172. Japanese gymnast Shun Fujimoto performed on a broken right knee, and helped the Japanese team win the gold medal for the team championship. He scored a ... thus securing gold for Japan.

a) 9.2 b) 9.7 c) 9.4 d) 9.8

1980 Olympics

173. How many countries participated in the Moscow Olympics?

a) *56* b) *80* c) *92* d) *112*

174. Although approximately half of the 24 countries which boycotted the 1976 Summer Olympics participated in these, the Games were disrupted by another, even larger, boycott led by the ... followed by 64 other countries in protest of the 1979 Soviet invasion of Afghanistan.

a) *Britain* b) *Canada*
c) *USA* d) *Australia*

175. As a form of protest against the USSR intervention in Afghanistan, how many countries marched in the Opening Ceremony with the Olympic Flag instead of their national flags, and the Olympic Flag and Olympic Hymn were used at Medal Ceremonies when athletes from these countries won medals?

a) *15* b) *13* c) *10* d) *5*

176. Of the competitors how many per cent were female — a higher percentage than at any previous Olympics?

a) *15* b) *17* c) *19* d) *21*

177. During the opening ceremony, Salyut 6 crew Leonid Popov and Valery Ryumin sent their greetings to the Olympians and wished them happy starts in the live communication between the station and the.... They appeared on the stadium's scoreboard and their voices were translated via loud speakers.

a) *Lokomotiv* b) *Luzhniki*
c) *Central Lenin Stadium* d) *Dinamo*

178. Women's field hockey was an Olympic sport for the first time. Six countries competed: Austria, India, Poland, Czechoslovakia, USSR and Zimbabwe. The gold medal was won by the team of which country ahead of the firm favourites of the USSR who won the bronze?

a) *Poland* b) *Austria*
c) *Zimbabwe* d) *Czechoslovakia*

179. India won a record ... title in men's field hockey.

a) *9th* b) *8th* c) *7th* d) *6th*

180. Which country beat the USSR 23-22 in the handball final to take their first medal of any sort in the men's event?

a) *East Germany* b) *France*
c) *Canada* d) *Belgium*

181. Which country won a bronze medal in water polo? This continued their run of always winning a medal in this event since 1924.

a) *Canada* b) *USA*
c) *Hungary* d) *Italy*

182. Name the mascot flying into the sky at the closing ceremony.

a) *Hodori, the tiger* b) *Misha, the bear cub*
c) *Sam, the eagle* d) *Olly, the kookaburra*

183. Which of these events did not produce a European record in 1980?

a) *Men's High Jump* b) *Men's Triple Jump*
c) *Men's Pole Vault* d) *Men's Long Jump*

184. What was the nationality of the 1980 women's 400m Olympic champion Marita Koch?

a) *Czech* b) *East German*
c) *Albanian* d) *Russian*

185. Why did Tolossa Kotu not win the 5000 metres in 1980?

a) *He missed the start.*
b) *He ran only in the 10,000 metres.*
c) *Aleksandr Fedotkin ran into the back of him on the last lap.*
d) *His shoe disintegrated going round the final bend.*

1984 Olympics

186. In view of the American-led boycott of the 1980 Summer Olympics in Moscow, the Soviet-led boycott of the 1984 Summer Olympics caused 14 Eastern Bloc countries and allies

including the Soviet Union, Cuba and East Germany (but not Romania) to boycott these Olympics. For differing reasons, Iran and which other country also boycotted?

a) *Jordon* b) *Kuwait*
c) *Libya* d) *Iraq*

187. The famous ... composer Sergio Mendes also composed a special song for the 1984 Olympic Games *Olympia* from his 1984 album *Confetti*.

a) *Brazilian* b) *Spanish*
c) *Mexican* d) *Canadian*

188. Nawal El Moutawakel of ... became the first female Olympic champion of an Islamic nation, and the first of her country in the 400 m hurdles.

a) *Sierra Leone* b) *Zambia*
c) *Chad* d) *Morocco*

189. Which sport returned for the first time since the 1924 Summer Olympics, this time as a demonstration sport?

a) *Badminton* b) *Golf*
c) *Tennis* d) *Cycling*

190. Professional wrestler Samoa Joe (then aged 5) appeared at the opening ceremony as a ....

a) *Singer* b) *Dancer*
c) *Flag bearer* d) *Drummer*

191. Where were the opening and closing ceremonies held?

a) *Dodger Stadium* b) *Athletes Village*
c) *Los Angeles Memorial Coliseum*
d) *Olympic Village*

1988 Olympics

192. Name the host city of the 1988 Olympics.

a) *Seoul, South Korea* b) *Tokyo, Japan*
c) *Beijing, China* d) *Atlanta, USA*

193. Who took the Judge's Oath?

a) *Hur Jae* b) *Sohn Kee-chung*
c) *Chung Sunman* d) *Lee Hakrae*

194. Anthony Nesty of ... won his country's first Olympic medal by winning the 100 m butterfly, scoring an upset victory over Matt Biondi by .01 of a second; he is also the first black person to win a swimming title.

a) *Chad* b) *Madagascar*
c) *Suriname* d) *Congo*

195. Table tennis was introduced at the Olympics, with ... and the host nation both winning two titles.

a) *China* b) *Japan* c) *Indonesia* d) *Vietnam*

1992 Olympics

196. What city's archery team lit up the cauldron with a flaming arrow in 1992?

a) *Paris* b) *Barcelona*
c) *London* d) *Myanmar*

197. Who were the only people allowed to compete in Biathlon until 1992?

a) *Men* b) *Women*
c) *Disabled* d) *People over 40 years of age*

198. South Africa was allowed again to participate in the Olympics after a ... years suspension in the Olympic Games for its apartheid policy.

a) *20* b) *24* c) *28* d) *32*

199. A novelty of these Games was that the cauldron was lit by Paralympics archer Antonio Rebellio by releasing a burning ....

a) *Arrow* b) *Wand*
c) *Ball* d) *Splint*

200. A then record number of ... nations won medals in Barcelona, including America through their basketball Dream Team, including the likes of Michael Jordan.

a) *54* b) *64* c) *74* d) *84*

201. China and ... were both heavily criticised for failing to take part in international drugs testing prior to the Games.

a) *Japan* b) *Indonesia*
c) *Malaysia* d) *Cuba*

202. Even ... joined the opening ceremony despite not having any athletes participating in the Games.

a) *Moscow* b) *Israel*
c) *Afghanistan* d) *Argentina*

203. A ... designer with an international reputation, Philippe Starck, was responsible for the design of the torch; this was a first in the history of the Olympic Games. Made in stainless steel, the torch had to be a rare object of value.

a) *British* b) *Canadian*
c) *Venezuelan* d) *French*

204. The Valencian artist, Javier Mariscal, created the ... as official mascot of the 1992 Barcelona Olympic Games.

a) *Tiger Hodori* b) *Kookaburra Olly*
c) *Dog Cobi* d) *Bear Misha*

1996 Olympics

205. In the 1996 rowing men's eight in Atlanta, which country grabbed the gold?

a) *Germany* b) *Great Britain*
c) *Russia* d) *Netherlands*

206. In women's basketball, who was the winning team in Atlanta?

a) *USA* b) *Australia*
c) *Brazil* d) *Croatia*

207. The ladies also played soccer in Atlanta. Which country was defending its title in Sydney?

a) *China* b) *Sweden*
c) *Norway* d) *USA*

2000 Olympics

208. Who read the Athlete's oath at the Opening Ceremony of the Sydney 2000 Games?

a) *Cathy Freeman* b) *Rachelle Hawkes*
c) *Andrew Gaze* d) *Kieren Perkins*

209. In the 2000 Sydney Olympics, how many official mascots were there?

a) *1* b) *4* c) *2* d) *3*

210. Which popular Australin singer sang the song *The Flame*, prior the the Olympic torch entering the stadium in 2000?

a) *Tina Arena* b) *Olivia Newton John*
c) *John Farnham* d) *Julie Anthony*

211. What sport did the reader of the athlete's oath at Sydney 2000 particpate in?

a) *Basketball* c) *Swimming*
c) *Football* d) *Hockey*

212. What is the name of Margie Goldstein-Engle's mount for the Sydney Olympic Games?

a) *Clasiko* b) *Rythmical*
c) *Hidden Creek's Perin* d) *Liberty*

213. In archery, who won the men's team final at the 2000 Olympics?

a) *Taiwan* b) *South Korea*
c) *Korea* d) *North Korea*

214. The first medal ever for a winner in an Olympic triathalon was won by Brigitte McMahon in 2000. From which country does she hail?

a) *Australia* b) *Canada*
c) *United Kingdom* d) *Switzerland*

215. In swimming, men 4x100 metre freestyle relay, the gold medal was won by Australia and the silver medal by the United States in 2000. Who was the winner of the bronze medal?

a) *The Netherlands* b) *Brazil*
c) *Germany* d) *Italy*

216. In triathalon the silver medal was won by Stefan Vuckovic in the 2000 Olympics. From which country does he hail?

a) *Czech Republic* b) *Yugoslavia*
c) *Germany* d) *Croatia*

217. The gold medal in fencing, men team epee, was won by which country in the 2000 Olympics?

a) *Cuba* b) *France*
c) *Italy* d) *Hungary*

218. The gold medal in gymnastics, men's team, was won by which country?

a) *Ukraine* b) *Russia*
c) *Japan* d) *China*

219. In women's softball, which country was the defending champion in Sydney?

a) *China* b) *Cuba*
c) *Australia* d) *USA*

220. In men's baseball in 2000, the defending Olympic champions were ....

a) *Japan* b) *China*
c) *USA* d) *Cuba*

221. Name the flag bearer who led the Australian team into the Opening Ceremony in 2000.

a) *Andrew Hoy* b) *Cathy Freeman*
c) *Andrew Gaze* d) *Keiran Perkins*

222. Where in Sydney were the majority of Olympic 2000 events held?

a) *Homebush Bay* b) *Brisbane*
c) *Darling Harbour* d) *Bondi*

223. Halil Mutlu won the gold medal in weightlifting, men's bantamweight in 2000. From what country is Halil Mutlu?

a) *Bulgaria* b) *Slovakia*
c) *Uzbekistan* d) *Turkey*

224. In 2000, in swimming, men's 400 m individual medley, the gold and silver medal went to swimmers from the same country. What country is that?

a) *Germany* b) *Canada*

c) *USA* d) *China*

225. Driulys Gonzalez won a silver medal in judo, women's lightweight in the 2000 Olympics. From what country is she?

a) *Spain* b) *Venezuela*

c) *Colombia* d) *Cuba*

226. What was the only sport played outside of the Sydney Region during the Sydney 2000 Olympics?

a) *Shooting* b) *Sailing*

c) *Football* d) *Tennis*

227. In fencing, men's individual epee, the gold medal was won by Pavel Kolobkov in 2000. From what country is Pavel Kolobkov?

a) *Estonia* b) *Ukraine*

c) *Belarus* d) *Russia*

228. In cycling, men's Olympic sprint, the gold medal was won by which country in 2000?

a) *The Netherlands* b) *United Kingdom*

c) *France* d) *Australia*

229. How many gold medals did Greece win in the Sydney 2000 Olympics?

a) *0* b) *12*

c) *4* d) *8*

230. In swimming men's 4x100 m freestyle, which country was the defending champion in Sydney?

a) *Russia* b) *USA*

c) *Germany* d) *Netherlands*

2004 OLYMPICS

231. Which country won the most medals in the Athens 2004 Olympics?

a) *China*
b) *Australia*
c) *Russia*
d) *USA*

232. Two countries were in the Olympics for the first time in 2004 Athens Olympics. Which were they?

a) *Kuwait and Qatar*
b) *Qatar and Kiribati*
c) *Kiribati and Timor-Leste*
d) *Timor-Leste and Kuwait*

233. How many medals had Greece received by the end of the Games in 2004?

a) *46*
b) *16*
c) *14*
d) *32*

234. What was the score after 12 rounds of the archery semi-final between Yamamoto of Japan and Cuddihy of Australia in 2004?

a) *112-112*
b) *114-114*
c) *115-115*
d) *113-113*

235. American Joanna Hayes won the women's 100m hurdles final in 2004. What wild thing happened during that race?

a) *The crowd kept interrupting the race by booing.*
b) *A racer stumbled over one of the hurdles.*
c) *A person from the crowd jumped one of the racers.*
d) *One of the racers fell down unconscious after winning a medal.*

236. Paul Hamm's men's individual all-around gymnastics gold medal in 2004 was under some controversy. In which other event did he participate that also had some controversy?

a) *The pommel horse event*
b) *The still rings event*
c) *The high bar event*
d) *The parallel bars event*

237. How many nations secured more than 30 gold medals during the 2004 Olympics?

a) *3* b) *5* c) *4* d) *2*

238. Which nation secured both individual gymnastic all-around gold medals in 2004?

a) *USA* b) *Japan*
c) *Russia* d) *Ukraine*

239. The Romanian men's team came to the Olympic Games wanting to prove that they were as good as their woman's team. Which medal did they win?

a) *Gold* b) *Did not win a medal*
c) *Silver* d) *Bronze*

240. In which event did the United States women win two medals in the individual competition?

a) *Balance beam* b) *Uneven bars*
c) *Floor exercise* d) *Vault*

241. Which team won the most combined medals in the men's and women's gymnastic competition in the 2004 Olympics?

a) *Japan* b) *Russia*
c) *Romania* d) *United States*

242. In rowing, there were 14 gold medals won by 11 different nations in 2004. Which two nations scooped more than one each?

a) *Great Britain & Australia*
b) *Russia & Poland* c) *New Zealand & France*
d) *Romania & Germany*

243. Which two nations won the hockey gold medals, women and men, in 2004?

a) *Holland & Pakistan* b) *Spain & Germany*
c) *India & Great Britain* d) *Germany & Australia*

244. In badminton, which country won the most gold medals?

a) *South Korea* b) *Denmark*
c) *Indonesia* d) *China*

245. The marathon is run over 42.195 km (26 miles and 385 yards). Where did this distance originate?

a) *Distance from Marathon to Athens*

b) *1908 Games in London*

c) *Paris to Versailles*

d) *1896 Games in Athens*

246. In the ancient Games, dating back to the year 776 BC, what was the distance of the original race, called the 'stade'?

a) *1500 metres*

b) *192.2 metres*

c) *Marathon distance*

d) *55 metres*

247. What cities missed out in the final selection for hosting the 2004 Olympic Games?

a) *Buenos Aires, Cape Town, Stockholm & Toronto*

b) *Beijing, Buenos Aires, Rome & Toronto*

c) *Beijing, Cape Town, Rome & Stockholm*

d) *Buenos Aires, Cape Town, Rome & Stockholm*

248. Which of the following US teams did not win a medal at the Athens games?

a) *The women's water polo team*

b) *The women's volleyball team*

c) *The women's synchronised swim team*

d) *The women's gymnastics team*

249. Which of the following sports events did not take place while the 2004 Olympics were going on?

a) *All of these took place at the same time as the Olympics*

b) *The Little League World Series*

c) *The US Open in tennis*

d) *The PGA Championship*

250. What was the track race that was delayed for a long time in 2004 because the Greek crowd was booing?

a) *Men's 200 m*

b) *Men's 100 m*

c) *Men's 100 m hurdles*

d) *Men's 4 X 100 m relay*

251. The world champions of basketball, Serbia and Montenegro, were beaten by which minnow on day six of the 2004 games, 90-87?

a) *New Zealand* b) *Costa Rica*

c) *Puerto Rico* d) *Australia*

252. South Africa broke the world record in the final of the men's 4 x 100 metre swimming relay in 2004. Which country held the record that the South Africans broke?

a) *United States* b) *Australia*

c) *Russia* d) *Mongolia*

253. When did the games in Athens 2004 take place?

a) *August 14th to 28th*

b) *August 10th to 25th*

c) *August 13th to 29th*

d) *August 13th to 30th*

254. USA won the most medals at the 2004 Olympics with over 100 combined. The USA won the most gold medals with 35, the most silver medals with [illegible] but did not win the most bronze. Which country won the most bronze medals?

a) *Japan* b) *Russia* c) *China* d) *Australia*

255. Which country won the gold medal in 2004 for baseball for the third time in the 4 times baseball was an Olympic sport?

a) *United States* b) *Cuba* c) *Australia* d) *Japan*

256. What medal did the United States win in men's basketball in 2004?

a) *Gold* b) *Bronze*

c) *Silver*

d) *They didn't win a medal in men's basketball*

257. In the swimming competition in 2004, the USA won 28 medals and came in first place. Which country was second?

a) *Australia* b) *Netherlands*

c) *Japan* d) *France*

258. Yana Klochkova, the gold medalist in the women's 400 and 200 metre swimming individual medley in 2004, represented which country?

a) *Bulgaria* b) *Russia*

c) *Ukraine* d) *Romania*

259. The women's soccer, basketball and softball teams, all won gold medals. Their male counterparts did not do as good. Which of the following did not play in the Athens 2004 Games?

a) *The US men's basketball team*

b) *The US volleyball team*

c) *The US men's soccer team*

d) *The US baseball team*

260. Who won the Olympic football gold?

a) *Paraguay* b) *Argentina* c) *Italy* d) *Iraq*

5

Winter Olympics

1. At which Winter Olympics did British ski jumper Eddie 'The Eagle' Edwards hit the headlines?

a) *Nagano 1998*
b) *Calgary 1988*
c) *Lillehammer 1994*
d) *Sapporo*

2. In what year were the first Winter Olympic Games conducted?

a) *296 BC*
b) *1824*
c) *1896*
d) *1924*

3. Which US speed skater won a gold medal and a set a world record at the 2002 Winter Olympics in Salt Lake City?

a) *Apolo Ohno*
b) *Jennifer Rodriguez*
c) *Alex Rodriguez*
d) *Derek Parra*

4. In which city were the first Winter Olympic Games held?

a) *Sokoto, Nigeria*
b) *Sapporo, Japan*
c) *Olympia, Greece*
d) *Chamonix-Mont-Blanc, France*

5. The 2002 Salt Lake City games were the ... Winter Olympics.

a) *18th*
b) *19th*
c) *20th*
d) *21st*

6. How many players on the United States Team played for Boston University in 1980 at the Lake Placid Winter Olympics?

a) 3
b) 4
c) 2
d) 5

7. **For which country did Ekaterina Dafovska cover 15 km on skis whilst also showing her shooting proficiency at the 1998 Nagano Games?**

    a) *Bulgaria* b) *Ukraine*
    c) *Russia* d) *Romania*

8. **Which country won the most medals with 35 total medals in the 2000 Salt Lake Games?**

    a) *USA* b) *Norway*
    c) *Germany* d) *Russia*

9. **Johann Muehlegg won three gold medals in cross-country skiing. He failed a drug test and one of his medals was removed. Which country did this athlete represent at the Salt Lake City 2000 Games?**

    a) *Germany* b) *Norway*
    c) *Austria* d) *Spain*

10. **Which of the following tricks was Michelle Kwan attempting when she had that highly publicised fall in her first practice in Torino 2006?**

    a) *A triple flip* b) *A triple lutz*
    c) *A triple axel* d) *A triple salcow*

11. **When was the Torino 2006 Olympic Winter Games held?**

    a) *February 12 - February 28*
    b) *February 10 - February 19*
    c) *February 17 - February 26*
    d) *February 10 - February 26*

12. **How many gold medals has Britain won in the Winter Olympics history?**

    a) *4* b) *6*
    c) *8* d) *9*

13. **The 1924 Winter Olympics closed with a ceremony honouring achievement in a non-Olympic sport. Which was it?**

    a) *Ice fishing* b) *Mountaineering*
    c) *Ptarmigan hunting* d) *Skydiving*

14. What is US Olympic skier, Resi Stiegler, known for wearing on top of her ski helmet?

a) *Kitty ears* b) *Pig's ears*

c) *A fruit basket* d) *Devil horns*

15. Why was the International Olympic Committee initially reluctant to create the Winter Olympics?

a) *Ice hockey was considered too violent.*

b) *Committee members were unfamiliar with most winter sports.*

c) *Most countries are too warm to host the Winter Games.*

d) *Early cameras and recording equipment were easily damaged by cold weather.*

16. Where was the 1988 Winter Olympics held?

a) *Nagano, Japan* b) *Lake Placid, USA*

c) *Calgary, Canada* d) *Lillehammer, Norway*

17. What caused British skier Alain Baxter's downfall at the 2002 Salt Lake City Games?

a) *Vicks* b) *Night Nurse*

c) *Sudafed* d) *Snow*

18. Anders Haugen (1888-1984), a Norwegian-born American, took third place in the special ski-jumping event at the 1924 Winter Olympics. However, he did not take home a bronze medal. Why not?

a) *He rejected the medal as a political protest.*

b) *He was discovered to have a criminal record.*

c) *The medal was awarded to a rival in error.*

d) *The medal was stolen from the hotel safe.*

19. Which of these NHL hockey stars was part of the US Olympic hockey team at the 2006 Winter Olympics?

a) *Jarome Iginla* b) *Sidney Crosby*

c) *Jeremy Roenick* d) *Mike Modano*

20. This speed skater won gold medals at the 1988, 1992, and 1994 Winter Olympics. Who is this?

a) *Gunda Niemann* b) *Jaap Eden*
c) *Bonnie Blair* d) *Eric Heiden*

21. How many times did Lake Placid host the Winter Olympics, in the 20th century?

a) *1* b) *0* c) *3* d) *2*

22. Where was the first official Winter Olympics held?

a) *Chamonix in France* b) *Aviemore in Scotland*
c) *Innsbruck in Austria* d) *Sokoto, Nigeria*

23. This female figure skater won the gold medal at three consecutive Winter Olympics, won the world championship on ten straight occasions, then went on to a long and lucrative show business career. Who was she?

a) *Madge Syers-Cave* b) *Katarina Witt*
c) *Peggy Fleming* d) *Sonja Henie*

24. Which winter Olympic sport does American speedster, Tony Benshoof, hold a world record?

a) *Short track speed skating* b) *Snowman building*
c) *Alpine skiing* d) *Luge*

25. Which Olympic figure skater was known for her camel?

a) *Sonja Henie* b) *Kristi Yamaguchi*
c) *Dorothy Hamill* d) *Tonya Harding*

26. Who won the rights to host the 20th Winter Olympics in 2006?

a) *Beijing, China* b) *Vancouver, Canada*
c) *Torino, Italy* d) *Salzburg, Austria*

27. Which of these disciplines made its Winter Olympics debut at the 2006 Games in Turin?

a) *Ski cross* b) *Snowboard cross*
c) *Cross-country skiing* d) *Water skiing*

28. Who or what is the "Skeleton"?

a) *A high-speed, face-down, head-first sledding event*
b) *Any member of the on-site physiotherapy staff*
c) *Kurt Kreisler, a notoriously thin Alpine skier*
d) *The slowest skier in the giant slalom*

29. Vonetta Flowers was the first African-American athlete to win a gold medal at the Winter Olympics. In what sport did he win a gold medal at the 2002 Winter Olympics?

a) *Figure Skating*
b) *Ice hockey*
c) *Cross-country skiing*
d) *Bobsleigh*

30. The mascots of the 2006 Winter Olympic Games in Turin, Italy, were ....

a) *A penguin and a reindeer*
b) *A polar bear and a snowshoe rabbit*
c) *A female snowball and a male ice cube*
d) *A moon and a sun*

31. What was the name of the American speed skater who captured the hearts of many during the Salt Lake City games, with a gold medal performance?

a) *Mark Anton Ohno*
b) *Apolo Anton Okoll*
c) *Apolo Archie Ohno*
d) *Apolo Anton Ohno*

32. Who was the last player cut from the 1980 US team?

a) *Les Auge*
b) *Ralph Cox*
c) *Jack Hughes*
d) *Bruce Horsch*

33. Bart Veldkamp had previously competed for his native country, but changed allegiance for the 1998 Winter Games. Which of these countries did he represent in that year?

a) *Netherlands*
b) *Belgium*
c) *Germany*
d) *Australia*

34. Jamie Sale and David Pelletier were the talk of the 2002 Olympics (the first week of competition in particular). What was their sport?

a) *Figure skating*
b) *Hockey*
c) *Bobsled*
d) *Curling*

35. Name the sport in which Switzerland's Simon Ammann won two gold medals in the 2002 Winter Games.

a) *Skeleton* b) *Downhill skiing*
c) *Ski jumping* d) *Biathlon*

36. Where are the 2010 Games being held?

a) *Vancouver, Canada* b) *Calgary, Canada*
c) *Montreal, Canada* d) *Ontario, Canada*

37. The 1932 Winter Olympics were held in Lake Placid, New York. The Japanese, new to alpine sports, finished out of the medals, but performed gamely. During the 50 km (31 mi.) ski race, one of their coaches used an unusual technique to inspire his team. What was it?

a) *Gave each racer a secret haiku to recite while skiing.*
b) *Made each skier carry a photo of the Emperor.*
c) *Played them the Japanese anthem at the hardest part of the course.*
d) *Promised to introduce them to American ice-cream.*

38. Which snowboarder won a gold medal in half pipe snowboarding at the 2002 Winter Olympics?

a) *Danny Kass* b) *J.J. Thomas*
c) *Ross Powers* d) *Shaun White*

39. Who won the 2002 gold in Olympic men's hockey?

a) *USA* b) *Canada*
c) *Czech Republic* d) *Russia*

40. Name the sport in which Fiona McDonald, Debbie Knox and Rhona Martin won a medal at the 2002 Olympic Games.

a) *Hockey* b) *Curling*
c) *Cross-Country Skiing* d) *Biathlon*

41. Which country topped the medal table at the 2002 Games?

a) *USA* b) *Austria*
c) *Germany* d) *Canada*

42. The biathlon is a hybrid sport in which flat-out cross-country skiing alternates with target shooting using a .22 rifle. The name biathlon dates to 1955. What had the sport previously been called?

a) *Ice soldier* b) *Kipplek*
c) *Patrol race* d) *Vinterfusil*

43. Which US figure skate competed in the Winter Olympics for the third time in 2006?

a) *Michelle Kwan* b) *Sarah Hughes*
c) *Timothy Goebel* d) *Sasha Cohen*

44. Which two men led Vancouver's bid for the 2010 Winter Olympics?

a) *Mike Furlong and John Poole*
b) *John Furlong and Jack Poole*
c) *Jack Furlong and John Poole*
d) *Jach Furlong and Mike Poole*

45. Which Winter Olympic sport uses a house and a stone?

a) *Ice hockey* b) *Curling*
c) *Biathlon* d) *Luge*

46. The USSR entered the Winter Olympics for the first time in 1956, and immediately made its presence felt by winning more medals than any other nation. They repeated this feat in 1960 and 1964, but not in 1968, when the run was broken by which nation?

a) *Canada* b) *France*
c) *Norway* d) *United States*

47. Freestyle skier, Toby Dawson, was flying over major moguls at the 2006 Winter Olympics. What is Toby's nickname?

a) *Captain Mogul* b) *Terrific Toby*
c) *Awesome Dawson* d) *Daring Dawson*

48. In Salt Lake 2002 Winter Olympics, which country won gold medals in both men's and women's hockey competitions?

a) *USA* b) *Sweden*
c) *Russia* d) *Canada*

49. In 1980, Lake Placid Winter Olympics, who was the oldest player on the United States team?

a) *Mike Eruzione* b) *Buzz Schneider*
c) *Jim Craig* d) *Steve Janazak*

50. In the Winter Olympics in Nagano, Japan in 1998, Elena Petrova used her skis and rifle to win silver for which country?

a) *Russia* b) *Germany*
c) *Belarus* d) *Ukraine*

51. In Salt Lake 2002 Winter Olympics, how many gold medals did the USA win?

a) *9* b) *12* c) *11* d) *10*

52. In Salt Lake 2002 Winter Olympics, Germany won the gold medal in the women's cross-country skiing relay competition and Norway won the silver medal. Which country won the bronze medal?

a) *Switzerland* b) *USA*
c) *Russia* d) *Austria*

53. The 1994 Winter Olympics were the first held between Summer Olympics rather than in the same year. They were also notable for the performance of Norwegian speed skater Johan Olav Koss. What did Koss do?

a) *Became the father of twins during the 10,000-meter race.*
b) *Broke the world record in three different events.*
c) *Won all five available gold medals.*
d) *Won his event after doctors said he wouldn't skate again.*

54. In 1980, Lake Placid Winter Olympics, what were the sprints that Herb made the players do at the end of the Norway game?

a) *Icies* b) *Herbies*
c) *Skaties* d) *Brooksies*

55. In the Winter Olympics in Nagano, Japan in 1998, Zali Stegall made her way down the mountainside quickly enough to bring some joy to her country. Which one?

a) *Australia* b) *Austria*
c) *Switzerland* d) *Germany*

56. **In Salt Lake 2002 Winter Olympics, which country won the gold medal for the men's 4-man bobsleigh event?**

a) *Germany* b) *Norway*
c) *USA* d) *Switzerland*

57. **In the 2006 Torino Olympics, the ice dancing competition made headlines one night because multiple competitors were falling on the ice. Which dance was being performed that night?**

a) *The break dance* b) *The free dance*
c) *The original dance* d) *The compulsory dance*

58. **What is Britain's best finish in a ski discipline at the Winter Olympics?**

a) *8th* b) *6th* c) *4th* d) *7th*

59. **The city of Torino, or Turin, was the site of the 2006 Winter Olympics. Turin has many other claims to fame, including its chocolate, its architecture, its Fiat plant, and all but one of the following. Which?**

a) *Destroyed by an arch-enemy of ancient Rome*
b) *First growing place of the distinctive uva blu wine*
c) *Home of a celebrated and controversial religious relic*
d) *Home town of a powerful Indian political leader*

60. **Which US snowboarder was a favourite to bring home a gold medal in snowboarder cross at the 2006 Winter Olympics?**

a) *Tara Dakides* b) *Elena Hight*
c) *Hannah Teter* d) *Lindsey Jacobellis*

61. **What two events does the biathlon combine?**

a) *Downhill skiing and ski jumping*
b) *Snowshoeing and fishing*
c) *Skiing and running*
d) *Cross-country skiing and shooting*

62. **Who is the youngest athlete ever to win a gold medal in the Winter Olympics?**

a) *Michelle Kwan* b) *Sonja Henie*
c) *Sarah Hughes* d) *Tara Lipinski*

63. In 1980, Lake Placid Winter Olympics, who was the goaltender that was cut from the team?

a) *Les Auge*
b) *Bruce Horsch*
c) *Dave Delich*
d) *Howard Hughes*

64. In the Winter Olympics in Nagano, Japan in 1998, Sean Olsson was a serving soldier when he (and some teammates) won a medal at Nagano. In which country's army was he serving?

a) *Canada*
b) *Great Britain*
c) *Sweden*
d) *Norway*

65. In Salt Lake 2002 Winter Olympics, who won the woman's curling final?

a) *USA*
b) *Canada*
c) *Great Britain*
d) *Switzerland*

66. How many gold medals did the United States win at the 2002 Winter Olympics in Salt Lake City?

a) *15*
b) *12*
c) *7*
d) *10*

67. In 1980, Lake Placid Winter Olympics, what was the name of the youngest player on the Soviet team (at the time of the games)?

a) *Alexei Kasatonov*
b) *Valeri Kharlamov*
c) *Vladimir Krutov*
d) *Vladislav Tretiak*

68. In Salt Lake 2002 Winter Olympics, which country won the men's curling event?

a) *Finland*
b) *Canada*
c) *Norway*
d) *Sweden*

69. Where were the 21st Olympic Winter Games scheduled to be held?

a) *France*
b) *Sweden*
c) *Finland*
d) *Canada*

70. In 2006, which country took home the bronze for the final 5000 metre men's relay speed skating event?

a) *Sweden*
b) *Canada*
c) *Italy*
d) *USA*

71. **Which current monarch has competed in five Winter Olympics?**

    a) *King Carl Gustaf of Sweden*
    b) *King Juan Carlos of Spain*
    c) *Prince Albert of Monaco*
    d) *Prime Minister Fredrik Reinfeldt*

72. **In Salt Lake 2002 Winter Olympics, these two countries both won a total of two medals and both medals were gold. Name the two countries.**

    a) *Australia and Spain* b) *Great Britain and Japan*
    c) *China and Korea* d) *Sweden and Poland*

73. **Name the athlete who won four gold medals in Salt Lake City.**

    a) *Samppa Lajunen (Finland)*
    b) *Ole Einar Bjoerndalen (Norway)*
    c) *Marc Gagnon (Canada)* d) *Derek Parra (USA)*

74. **In the 2006 Torino Olympics, Tugba Karademir made history for being the first figure skating participant from her country. What country is she from?**

    a) *Turkey* b) *Iran*
    c) *Iraq* d) *Egypt*

75. **Which of the following terms does not relate to winter sports?**

    a) *Triple axel* b) *Halfpipe*
    c) *Icing* d) *Ice Cube*

6

Winners and Medals

1896 Olympics

1. **The athletic highlight for the Greeks was the marathon victory by their compatriot ....**

   a) *Spyros Samaras* b) *Kostis Palamas*
   c) *Spiridon Louis* d) *Carl Schuhmann*

2. **Who was the most successful competitor in terms of victories?**

   a) *Spyros Samaras* b) *Carl Schuhmann*
   c) *James Connelly* d) *Demetrios Bikilas*

3. **The curves of the track were very tight, making fast times in the running events virtually impossible. Despite this, who won both the 100 m and the 400 m for the US?**

   a) *Thomas Burke* b) *James Connelly*
   c) *Paul Masson* d) *Alfred Flatow*

4. **Who was the best cyclist on the track, winning the one lap time trial, the sprint event, and the 10,000 metres?**

   a) *Léon Flameng* b) *Aristidis Konstantinidis*
   c) *Adolf Schmal* d) *Paul Masson*

5. **Name the Austrian fencer Adolf Schmal won the 12 hours race.**

   a) *Carl Schuhmann* b) *Louis Zutter*
   c) *Léon Flameng* d) *Adolf Schmal*

6. **Who won the road race event?**

a) *Léon Flameng* b) *Aristidis Konstantinidis*
c) *Hermann Weingärtner* d) *Alfred Flatow*

7. **Which of the fencers became the first Greek modern Olympic champion by winning the masters foil competition?**

a) *Hermann Weingärtner* b) *Léon Flameng*
c) *Louis Zutter* d) *Leonidas Pyrgos*

8. **The foil event was won by a Frenchman name him.**

a) *Léon Flameng* b) *Friedrich Traun*
c) *Eugène-Henri Gravelotte* d) *Louis Zutter*

9. **Which gymnast, who also took two seconds and a third place, won the horizontal bar event?**

a) *Hermann Weingärtner* b) *Alfred Flatow*
c) *Carl Schuhmann* d) *Louis Zutter*

10. **Who won the parallel bars?**

a) *Hermann Weingärtner* b) *Alfred Flatow*
c) *Carl Schuhmann* d) *Louis Zutter*

11. **Which competitor, who also competed successfully in wrestling, won the vault?**

a) *Hermann Weingärtner* b) *Alfred Flatow*
c) *Carl Schuhmann* d) *Louis Zutter*

12. **Held at a shooting range at Kallithea, there were five shooting events—two rifle events and three pistol shooting competitions. The first event, for military rifles over 200 metres, was won by ..., the only competitor to hit the target with all of his shots.**

a) *Sumner Paine* b) *Ioannis Phrangoudis*
c) *Georgios Orphanidis* d) *Pantelis Karasevdas*

13. **... the first Olympic champion in swimming, is one of only two Olympians to have won medals in both sport and art competitions. Unlike today, the 1896 swimming competitions were held at open sea.**

a) *Paul Neumann* b) *Alfréd Hajós*
c) *Georgios Orphanidis* d) *Sumner Paine*

14. Weightlifting champion Launceston Elliot faced gymnastics champion Carl Schuhmann from .... The latter won easily and advanced into the final, where he met Georgios Tsitas. Their final match had to be abandoned after 40 minutes of wrestling when darkness fell in and was continued the following day, when Schuhmann finished the bout within a quarter of an hour.

a) *Germany* b) *Greece*
c) *Austria* d) *Hungary*

15. Irishman John Pius Boland, who was in Athens on holiday, had been entered in the competition by a Greek friend, and won relatively easily. In the first round, he defeated ..., a German who had been eliminated in the 800 m competition.

a) *Hubert van Innis* b) *Alfréd Hajós*
c) *Friedrich Traun* d) *Hermann Weingärtner*

1900 Olympics

16. Who won the 60 metres, the 110 metres, the 220 metre hurdles, and the long jump events? As of 2005, these four individual gold medals are still a record for a track and field athlete.

a) *Meyer Prinstein* b) *Alvin Kraenzlein*
c) *Albert Robert Ayat* d) *Hubert van Innis*

17. Who was the first woman to become Olympic champion after winning the women's singles tennis competition? She later went on to win the mixed doubles tournament.

a) *Heidi Schuler* b) *Stella Walsh*
c) *Anita Walman* d) *Charlotte Cooper*

18. Belgian Hubert van Innis took two gold medals and one silver and would add to his tally how many years later in Antwerp?

a) *Twelve* b) *Twenty*
c) *Four* d) *Eight*

19. The ... rider Giovanni Giorgio Trissino won a gold and a silver.

a) *Brazilian* b) *Ecuadorian*
c) *Sicilian* d) *Italian*

20. **... Konrad Stäheli was the outstanding marksman of the Games, taking a trio of titles and leading his country to the top of the shooting medal table.**

a) *Switzerland's* b) *Hungary's*
c) *Austria's* d) *Romania's*

21. **Athletes from Columbia University, Princeton University and the University of Pennsylvania all won gold medals. Alvin Kraenzlein won ... individual gold medals, a feat that has never repeated, while John Tewksbury took five medals including two golds.**

a) *Seven* b) *Six*
c) *Four* d) *Five*

22. **United States dominance in sprinting was matched in the longer track races by Great Britain. Only George Orton, who won ... first Olympic title in the shorter of the two steeplechases, ruined a perfect record for the British.**

a) *Canada's* b) *Australia's*
c) *New Zealand's* d) *South Africa's*

23. **The Hungarian ... Rudolf Bauer was the only non-American crowned as Olympic Champion.**

a) *Fencer* b) *Discus thrower*
c) *Gymnast* d) *Swimmer*

24. **Whose domination was even greater in the field events than the track events with outstanding performances coming from Ray Ewry and Irving Baxter?**

a) *Canadian* b) *Australian*
c) *British* d) *American*

25. **John Arthur Jarvis of Great Britain, Frederick Lane of Australia and the German Ernst Hoppenberg each won two titles in .... Lane received a 50-pound bronze statue of a horse as a prize.**

a) *Tennis* b) *Swimming*
c) *Athletics* d) *Equestrian*

1904 Olympics

26. One of the most remarkable athletes was the American gymnast George Eyser. How many medals did he win even though his left leg was made of wood?

a) *Three* b) *Four*
c) *Five* d) *Six*

27. Chicago runner Jim Lightbody won the ... and the 800 m and then set a world record in the 1500 m.

a) *100 m* b) *Steeplechase*
c) *Marathon* d) *Long Jump*

28. Who won both the 200 m and 400 m hurdles and also the flat 400 m?

a) *Harry Hillman* b) *Jim Lightbody*
c) *George Eyser* d) *Archie Hahn*

29. In the discus, after American Martin Sheridan had thrown exactly the same distance as his compatriot, ...(39.28 m), the judges gave them both an extra throw to decide the winner. Sheridan won the decider and claimed the gold medal.

a) *Ralph Rose* b) *Ray Ewry*
c) *Jim Lightbody* d) *George Eyser*

30. Sprinter Archie Hahn was champion in the 60 m, 100 m and 200 m. In this last race, he set a new Olympic record in 21.6, a record that stood for how many years?

a) *20* b) *24* c) *28* d) *32*

31. Who again won all three standing jumps?

a) *Archie Hahn* b) *George Eyser*
c) *Ray Ewry* d) *Martin Sheridan*

1908 Olympics

32. Oscar Swahn from Sweden, who won the gold medal for running deer shooting, became the oldest Olympic champion of all time, and set another age record by being ... years and

279 days old during his triumph at the 1920 Summer Olympics in Antwerp, Belgium.

a) *70* b) *72* c) *73* d) *75*

33. **Paul Radmilovic, nicknamed Pavao, he was a member of the champion water polo team and the best 4 x 200m freestyle relay. He also won gold medals in water polo in Stockholm (1912) and in Antwerp (1920).**

a) *Champ* b) *Flyer*
c) *Radmi* d) *Pavao*

34. **In the 400-m, three Americans defeated Halswelle of ..., but the judges ruled that one of the Americans had obstructed Halswelle, and was disqualified. The other tow Americans, in protest withdrew from the race, leaving Halswelle a solitary run to victory in a one-man race!**

a) *Holland* b) *Ireland*
c) *New Zealand* d) *England*

35. **In high jump, which American took the honours?**

a) *Leahy* b) *Porter*
c) *Somodi* d) *Andre*

1912 Olympics

36. **Who won the pentathlon and the newly created decathlon?**

a) *Jim Thorpe* b) *Oscar Swahn*
c) *Steve Redgrave* d) *Hannes Kolhemainen*

37. **Swedish marksman Oscar Swahn became the oldest Olympic gold medalist (up to that time), at the age of 64, in which event?**

a) *Field* b) *Deer-shooting*
c) *Track* d) *Gymnastic*

38. **Ewart Douglas Horsfall won his first two gold medals for in rowing for which country? He has widely been considered the country's greatest rower prior to Steve Redgrave.**

a) *Great Britain* b) *Canada*
c) *Australia* d) *South Africa*

39. **Hannes Kolhemainen became which country's first Olympic champion, winning the 5,000-m, 1000-m and 8,000-m cross-country?**

a) *Holland* b) *Finland*
c) *Denmark* d) *Belgium*

1920 Olynpics

40. **Duke Kahanamoku retained the ... swimming title he won before the war.**

a) *200 m* b) *400 m* c) *100 m* d) *800 m*

41. **How many gold medals did Nedo Nadi win in the fencing events?**

a) *Five* b) *Two* c) *Four* d) *Six*

42. **Twenty-three-year old Paavo Nurmi won the 10,000 m and 8,000 m cross country, took another gold in team cross country, and a silver in 5,000 m run. His contributions for which country broke the US dominance record in track and field with 9 medals?**

a) *Finland* b) *Switzerland*
c) *Denmark* d) *Hungary*

1924 Olympics

43. **The 'Flying Finns' dominated the long distance running whilst the British and Americans dominated the shorter events. Paavo Nurmi won the ... m and 5000 m (which were held with only an hour between them) and the cross country run (held in xtremely hot weather).**

a) *400 m* b) *800 m* c) *1500 m* d) *100 m*

44. **Who won the 10000 m and the 3000 m steeplechase, while finishing second to Nurmi on the 5000 m and cross country?**

a) *Harold Abrahams* b) *Eric Liddell*
c) *Ville Ritola* d) *Albin Stenroos*

45. **Albin Stenroos won the marathon, while ... the team was victorious in the 3000 m and cross country team events.**

a) *Finnish* b) *British*
c) *Hungarian* d) *Swiss*

46. **British runner Harold Abrahams won the gold in the ... m.**

a) *100* b) *200* c) *400* d) *800*

47. **Who won the gold medal in the 200 and 400 m?**

a) *Paavo Nurmi* b) *Eric Liddell*
c) *Harold Abrahams* d) *Albin Stenroos*

48. **Who won the 800 m?**

a) *Harold Abrahams* b) *Eric Liddell*
c) *Ville Ritola* d) *Douglas Lowe*

49. **Swimmer Johnny Weissmuller won three gold medals in swimming and one bronze in ....**

a) *High Jump* b) *Fencing*
c) *Water polo* d) *100 m*

50. **Fencer Roger Ducret of which country won five medals, of which three were gold?**

a) *Canada* b) *France*
c) *Brazil* d) *Venezuela*

51. **In gymnastics who scored a 10 here and also a perfect 10 on side vault?**

a) *Douglas Lowe* b) *Albin Stenroos*
c) *Albert Seguin* d) *Harold Abrahams*

1928 Olympics

52. **The winner of the triple jump in 1928 was the first gold medallist from his country at any Olympics. Who was he?**

a) *Ladislav Vacha of Czechoslovakia*
b) *Mikio Oda of Japan*
c) *Pat O'Callaghan of Ireland*
d) *Ted Morgan of New Zealand*

53. **The great Paavo Nurmi of Finland won one gold and two silver medals in the 1928 Games. Which event did he win?**

a) *Marathon* b) *5,000 metres*
c) *10,000 metres* d) *3,000 metre steeplechase*

54. Percy Williams of Canada won two gold medals. Which events did he win?

a) *100 and 200 metres* b) *Shot putt and discus*
c) *Long jump and decathlon* d) *400 and 800 metres*

1932 Olympics

55. Eddie Tolan of USA won which two track and field events?

a) *100 and 200 metres* b) *1500 and 5000 metres*
c) *400 and 800 metres* d) *Shot putt and discus*

56. Who won two gold medals in the javelin and the hurdles event, and competed in a jump-off for a third in the high jump? Her technique in the jump-off was ruled illegal, leaving her with second place.

a) *Babe Didrikson* b) *Stanislawa Walasiewicz*
c) *Helene Madison* d) *Maria Polonski*

57. Poland's Stanislawa Walasiewicz won the gold medal in the women's 100 metres; she would also win the silver medal in the event four years later. After her death in ..., it was discovered that she was intersex and would have been ineligible to participate.

a) *1956* b) *1872* c) *1980* d) *1964*

58. Finnish star Paavo Nurmi was barred from competing in the Olympics for being ....

a) *An amateur* b) *A drug addict*
c) *A professional* d) *A smoker*

59. Helene Madison won three gold medals in ....

a) *400 m* b) *High jump*
c) *Long jump* d) *Swimming*

60. Jim Thorpe took part in the Games as a ....

a) *Competitor* b) *Referee*
c) *Judge* d) *Press reporter*

1936 Olympics

61. In the cycling match sprint finals, the German Toni Merkens fouled Arie van Vliet of the Netherlands. Instead of disqualification he was fined ... marks and kept his gold.

a) *100* b) *500* c) *1,000* d) *2,000*

62. The African-American Jesse Owens won how many gold medals in the sprint and long jump events? His German competitor Lutz Long had offered Owens advice after he almost failed qualifying in the long jump and was posthumously awarded the Pierre de Coubertin medal for sportsmanship.

a) *Two* b) *Three*
c) *Four* d) *Five*

63. Rie Mastenbroek of ... won three gold medals and a silver in swimming. In the freestyle, swimmers originally dove from the pool walls, but diving blocks were eventually incorporated at the 1936 Olympics.

a) *Switzerland* b) *The Netherlands*
c) *Yugoslavia* d) *Belgium*

64. Rower Jack Beresford won his ... Olympic medal in the sport, and his third gold medal.

a) *Second* b) *Third*
c) *Fourth* d) *Fifth*

65. ... gymnasts Konrad Frey and Alfred Schwarzmann both won three gold medals.

a) *Austrian* b) *Bulgarian*
c) *Romanian* d) *German*

1948 Olympics

66. Fanny Blankers-Koen, a ..., became the first athlete to win an Olympic athletics title.

a) *Dutch* b) *Hungarian*
c) *Uruguayan* d) *South African*

67. **The dropping of Dillard from the hurdles did nothing to lessen America's domination. Who won in an Olympic record of 13.9 sec despite hitting three hurdles?**

a) *Clyde Scott* b) *Craig Dixon*
c) *Roy Cochran* d) *William Porter*

68. **The most striking American performance was from Robert Mathias, 17, taking part in just his third .... He went into the lead with three events left, threw the discus further than anyone else and then staggered round the 1,500 m to finish third but last, but with enough points to secure a gold medal.**

a) *Marathon* b) *Decathlon*
c) *Penthatlon* d) *5000 m*

69. **Who won the 400 m after setting an Olympic record in the semi-final?**

a) *Duncan White* b) *William Porter*
c) *Roy Cochran* d) *Clyde Scott*

70. **Duncan White of ... won the first medal for his country, a silver, in the 400 metre hurdles.**

a) *Ceylon* b) *Ireland*
c) *New Zealand* d) *West Indies*

1952 Olympics

71. **Rules in equestrianism now allowed non-military officers to compete, including women. Lis Hartel of ... became the first woman in the sport to win a medal.**

a) *Hungary* b) *Denmark*
c) *Belgium* d) *Holland*

72. **Emil Zátopek of Czechoslovakia won three gold medals in the 5,000m, 10,000m and which other event?**

a) *Marathon* b) *Pole vault*
c) *Swimming* d) *Canoeing*

73. **Bob Mathias of the USA became the first Olympian to successfully defend his decathlon title with a total score of how many points?**

a) *1,278* b) *4,987* c) *5,999* d) *7,887*

1956 Olympics

74. Who won both the men's 5 km as well as the 10 km in 1956?

a) *Ron Clark* b) *Vladimir Kuts*
c) *Emil Zatopek* d) *Mamo Wolde*

75. Who won the women's 1500 metres?

a) *Edith Szewinska*
b) *Ludmilla Bragina*
c) *This event wasn't run until 1972.*
d) *Linda Papp*

76. One of the few triple-jumpers who were able to prologue their Olympic title was this South-American, who won his second title in Melbourne. Who is it?

a) *Adhemar da Silva (BRA)*
b) *Joao Carlos De Oliveira (BRA)*
c) *Arnoldo Devonish (VEN)*
d) *Delfo Cabrera (ARG)*

77. Who was on the podium for the men's 200m dash?

a) *1. t. Courtney USA 2. D) Johnson GBR 3. A) Boysen NOR*
b) *1. BJ Morrow USA 2.T. Baker USA 3. H. Hogan AUS*
c) *1. BJ Morrow USA 2. A) Stanfield USA 3. T. Baker USA*
d) *1. C) Jenkins USA 2. KH Haas GER 3. V. Hellsten FIN*

78. Betty Cuthbert, an 18-year-old from ..., won the 100- and 200-metre dashes and ran a great final leg in the 4 x 100-meter relay to overcome Great Britain's lead and claim her third gold medal.

a) *Sydney* b) *Dunedin*
c) *New York* d) *Wellington*

79. Murray Rose became the first male ... swimmer to win two freestyle events since Johnny Weissmuller in 1924

a) *American* b) *Australian*
c) *Irish* d) *Canadian*

80. Who again took gold medals in both the springboard and the platform?

a) *Pat McCormick* b) *Bob Clotworthy*
c) *Gary Tobian* d) *Joaquim Capilla*

81. Tom Courtney barely overtook ... Derek Johnson in the 800-metre run, then collapsed from the exertion and needed medical attention.

a) *USA's* b) *Canada's*
c) *New Zealand's* d) *Great Britain's*

82. Which of Ireland's entrants ran a brilliant 53.8 over the last 400 metres to win the 1,500-metre run?

a) *John Landy* b) *Chris Brasher*
c) *Ron Delaney* d) *Gary Tobian*

83. Who became the first Briton to win a gold medal in track and field since 1932?

a) *Heinz Laufer* b) *Sandor Rozsnyoi*
c) *Ernst Larsen* d) *Chris Brasher*

84. Mildred McDaniel, the only American woman to win gold in the sport, set a high jump record of 5 feet, ... inches.

a) *8 1/4* b) *7 1/2* c) *9 1/2* d) *9 1/4*

85. Egil Danielsen of ... overcame a troublesome wind with a remarkable javelin throw of 281 feet, 2 1/2 inches.

a) *Norway* b) *Sweden*
c) *Finland* d) *Denmark*

1960 Olympics

86. Danish sailor Paul Elvstrøm won his ... straight gold medal in the Finn class. The only others to emulate his performance in an individual event are Al Oerter, Carl Lewis and, if the Intercalated Games of 1906 are included, Ray Ewry.

a) *Third* b) *Fourth*
c) *Fifth* d) *Sixth*

87. The future Constantine II, King of ..., won his country a gold in sailing Dragon Class.

a) *Greece* b) *Turkey*
c) *Yugoslavia* d) *Croatia*

88. Fencer Aladar Gerevich of ... won his sixth consecutive gold medal in the team sabre event (1932-1936, 1948-1960).

a) *Austria* b) *Hungary*
c) *Switzerland* d) *Poland*

89. Wilma Rudolph, a former ... patient, won three gold medals in sprint events on the track.

a) *Polio* b) *Asthma*
c) *Cancer* d) *Heart*

90. Abebe Bikila of Ethiopia won the marathon bare-footed to become the first black African Olympic champion although he specialised in the ... race.

a) *800 m* b) *1500 m*
c) *25 km* d) *5000 m*

91. ..., later known as Muhammad Ali, won boxing's light-heavyweight gold medal.

a) *Michael Johnson* b) *Michael Jackson*
c) *Cassius Clay* d) *Cassius Cay*

92. Swedish ... Gert Fredriksson won his sixth Olympic title.

a) *Fencer* b) *Swimmer*
c) *Canoer* d) *Rider*

93. Australian athlete Herb Elliott won the men's ... metres in one of the most dominating performances in Olympic history.

a) *200* b) *400*
c) *800* d) *1500*

94. American athlete Rafer Johnson defeated his rival and friend C.K. Yang in one of the greatest events in Olympic history.

a) *Marathon* b) *5000 m*
c) *Penthatlon* d) *Decathlon*

95. In which event did Jeff Farrell, US, win two gold medals after undergoing an emergency appendectomy six days before the Olympic Trials?

a) *Swimming* b) *Athletics*
c) *Gymanstics* d) *Equestrian*

1964 Olympics

96. Judo and volleyball, both popular sports in Japan, were introduced to the Olympics. Japan won three of the titles in judo, but ... Anton Geesink won the Open category.

a) *Swiss* b) *Dutchman*
c) *Hungarian* d) *Bulgarian*

97. Reigning world champion Osamu Watanabe capped off his career with a gold medal for Japan in freestyle wrestling, surrendering no points and retiring from competition as the only undefeated Olympic champion to date at ...

a) *189-0* b) *159-3*
c) *176-2* d) *192-1*

98. Soviet gymnast Larissa Latynina won two gold medals (both for the third time in a row in team competition and floor exercise events), a silver medal and two bronze medals. She ended her Olympic career and holds the record for most Olympic medals at ... since then.

a) *15* b) *16*
c) *18* d) *19*

99. ... swimmer Dawn Fraser won the 100 m freestyle event for the third time in a row, a feat matched by Vyacheslav Ivanov in rowing's single scull event.

a) *Australian* b) *British*
c) *Canadian* d) *American*

100. Bob Hayes won the 100 m title in a time of 10.0 seconds, equaling the world record. He had run the distance in . . . seconds in the semifinal but this was not recognised as a world record as it was wind assisted.

a) *9.9* b) *9.8*
c) *9.7* d) *9.6*

1968 Olympics

101. US discus thrower Al Oerter, won his . . . consecutive gold medal in the event to become only the athlete to achieve this feat in an individual event.

a) *First* b) *Second*
c) *Third* d) *Fourth*

102. After winning the gold medal for heavyweight boxing, who walked around the ring with a tiny American flag, bowing several times to the audience?

a) *Bob Beamon* b) *Roy Johnson*
c) *Ray Ewry* d) *George Foreman*

103. Gymnast Vera Cáslavská of which country won four gold medals?

a) *Poland* b) *Hungary*
c) *Czechoslovakia* d) *Russia*

104. Which United States swimmer became the first swimmer to win three individual gold medals in the 200, 400 and 800 m freestyle events?

a) *Laura Charles* b) *Vanessa Brighton*
c) *Debbie Meyer* d) *Mary Williams*

105. Bob Beamon jumped . . . in the long jump, a 55 cm improvement of the world record that would stand until 1991 (when it was broken by Mike Powell).

a) *7. 90* b) *8.70* c) *8.90* d) *9.20*

1972 Olympics

106. Name the swimmer from the United States who set a world record when he won seven gold medals (while on the way to setting a new world record for each of his seven gold medals) in a single Olympics, bringing his lifetime total to nine (he had won two golds in Mexico City's Games four years earlier).

a) *Vince Matthews* b) *Mark Spitz*
c) *Wayne Collett* d) *Edwin Moses*

107. Which tiny Soviet gymnast became a media star after winning a gold medal in the team competition event, failing to win in the individual all-around after a fall (she was beaten by Lyudmilla Turischeva), and finally winning two gold medals in the balance?

a) *Olga Korbut* b) *Heikki Savolainen*
c) *Heidi Schuler* d) *Nadia Comaneci*

108. Lasse Virén of ... won the 5,000 and 10,000 m (the latter after a fall), a feat he would repeat in the 1976 Summer Olympics.

a) *Sweden* b) *Norway*
c) *Finland* d) *Denmark*

109. Who won both the 100 m and 200 m in track and field events?

a) *Steve Prefontaine* b) *Valeri Borzov*
c) *Rey Robinson* d) *Eddie Hayes*

110. Also in track and field, two black American 400 m runners, Vincent Matthews and Wayne Collett, acted casually on the medal stand, twirling their medals (gold and silver, respectively) and joking with one another as 'The Star-Spangled Banner' was being played during the award ceremony. They were banned from the Olympics for how many years?

a) *Two* b) *Three* c) *Five* d) *Life*

1976 Olympics

111. 14-year-old Nadia Comaneci of which country scored seven perfect 10s and won three gold medals, including the prestigious All Around? The score board could hold only 3 digits and the score was shown as 1:00.

a) *Russia* b) *Hungary*
c) *Romania* d) *Yugoslavia*

112. In women's gymnastics three gold medals were also won by Nellie Kim. To which country did she belong?

a) *USSR* b) *Scotland*
c) *Ireland* d) *Austria*

113. Viktor Saneyev (Soviet Union) won his third consecutive triple jump gold medal, while Klaus Dibiasi did the same in the platform diving event. From where did Klaus hail?

a) *Russia* b) *Austria*
c) *Denmark* d) *Italy*

114. Alberto Juantorena of ... became the first man to win both the 400 m and 800 m at the same Olympics.

a) *Cuba* b) *Mexico*
c) *Brazil* d) *Afgentina*

115. Five American boxers - Sugar Ray Leonard, Leon Spinks, Michael Spinks, Leo Randolph and Howard Davis Jr.—won gold medals in boxing. This has been often called the greatest Olympic boxing team the United States ever had, and, out of the five American gold medalists in boxing, all but ... went on to become professional world champions.

a) *Davis* b) *Randolph*
c) *Spinks* d) *Leonard*

1980 Olympics

116. Who were the top four in the men's 1500?

a) *Ovett, Coe, Kirov, Guimaraes*
b) *Coe, Straub, Ovett, Busse*
c) *Coe, Ovett, Fontanella, Busse*
d) *Ovett, Busse, Coe, Cram*

117. Who coached the Russian Hammer champion Yuri Sedykh?

a) *Griva Maris* b) *Anatoli Bondarchuk*
c) *Nikolay Malishev* d) *Sergei Litvinov*

118. Who came fourth in the women's 100m?

a) *Ingrid Auerswald* b) *Stephanie Hightower*
c) *Heather Hunte* d) *Linda Haglund*

119. This man from Finland, who had not finished any of the previous 3 days shootings higher than 4th, came from 4th on the last day to win the men's archery competition, scoring 2455

points. He won gold just 3 points ahead of a Soviet. It was the equivalent of winning a marathon just a few paces ahead of a rival. What is his name?

a) *Gerd Wessig* b) *Wladyslaw Kozakiewicz*
c) *Tomi Poikolainen* d) *Anatoly Solomin*

120. Who won the women's archery gold and who was also the world, European and Soviet champion?

a) *Ketevan Losaberidze* b) *Natalia Butuzova*
c) *Tatiana Kolpakova* d) *Barbel Wockel*

121. Scotsman Allan Wells beat ... Silvio Leonard and became the first Briton since 1924 to win the Olympic 100 metres. It was the closest 100 m race at the Olympics in 28 years. It was a photo finish with both runners timed at 10.25 seconds.

a) *Cuban* b) *Mexican*
c) *Brazilian* d) *Sri Lankan*

122. Who retained the 1,500 m title that she had won in Montreal?

a) *Evelin Jahl* b) *Tatiana Kazankina*
c) *Maria Colon* d) *Sara Simeoni*

123. Who won the long jump gold? His was the longest jump recorded at sea level and he became only the 2nd human to jump further than 28 feet.

a) *Viktor Saneyev* b) *Yuri Sedykh*
c) *Lutz Dombrowski* d) *Dainis Kula*

124. Daley Thompson won the gold in the Decathlon. He won gold again at the L.A. Olympics. From where did he hail?

a) *Canada* b) *Great Britain*
c) *USA* d) *Australia*

125. Who became the first boxer to win three consecutive Olympic titles in heavyweight, the only boxer to win the same event in 3 Games?

a) *Patrizio Oliva* b) *Michael Anthonys*
c) *Teófilo Stevenson* d) *Sergei Postrekhin*

126. Robert Dill-Bundi became the 1st Olympic champion in the history of Swiss ....

a) *Cycling* b) *Skiing*
c) *Mountain climbing* d) *Rowing*

127. . . . (East Germany) was 4th after the preliminary high dives, behind 2 Soviets and a Mexican, but came back to win gold on the second day of competition.

a) *Irina Kalinina* b) *Olga Rukavishnikova*
c) *Nadezhda Tkachenko* d) *Martina Jaschke*

128. Who/was the oldest medallist at the Moscow Olympics was in the dressage at 57 years 283 days?

a) *Jan Kowalczyk* b) *Petre Rosca*
c) *Nikolai Koralkov* d) *Alexander Dityatin*

129. Name the East German pipping Nikolai Andrianov who had won gold on floor (gymnastics) at both Munich and Montreal.

a) *Zoltan Magyar* b) *Anatoly Starostin*
c) *Roland Bruckner* d) *George Horvath*

130. ... sailor Valentyn Mankin won a gold medal in 'Star' class. He won Olympic champion titles in 'Finn' and 'Tempest' classes before, and as of 2007 remains the only sailor in Olympic history to win gold medals in three different classes.

a) *Soviet* b) *Denmark*
c) *East German* d) *Polish*

131. The 3-day skeet shooting marathon was won by ... of Denmark, the 2nd Olympic gold for Danish shooters since the 1900 Paris Games.

a) *Hans Kjeld Rasmussen* b) *Karoly Varga*
c) *Vladimir Salnikov* d) *Backstroker Rica Reinisch*

132. Which Russian won three gold medals in swimming? He became the first man in history to break the magic 15 minute barrier in the 1500 metre freestyle, swimming's equivalent of breaking the 4-minute mile. He missed the LA Games because of the boycott but won gold again in this event at Seoul 1988.

a) *Hans Kjeld Rasmussen* b) *Karoly Varga*
c) *Vladimir Salnikov* d) *Backstroker Rica Reinisch*

133. Which Russian became the 1st middle weightlifter to clear more than 400 kg (lift and jerk).

a) *Karoly Varga* b) *Vladimir Salnikov*
c) *Yurik Vardanyan* d) *Backstroker Rica Reinisch*

134. In Graeco-Roman ... Ferenc Kocsis of Hungary was declared the winner of the 163 pound class when the Olympic and Soviet defending champion Anatoly Bykov was disqualified for passivity.

a) *Boxing* b) *Sparring*
c) *Karate* d) *Wrestling*

135. In the 106 pound freestyle wrestling final Italy's Claudio Pollio put Soviet . . . grappler and twice world champion to the mat to take an unexpected gold on point standings.

a) *Yurik Vardanyan* b) *Sergei Kornilaev*
c) *Vladimir Salnikov* d) *Hans Kjeld Rasmussen*

1984 Olympics

136. Carl Lewis made his first of four appearances in the Olympics, and equalled the performance of Jesse Owens of 1936, winning four gold medals in the 100 m, 200 m, 4x100 m relay and ....

a) *Long jump* b) *High jump*
c) *Steeplechase* d) *Hurdles*

137. Who set a new world record in winning the gold medal in the 200-metre breaststroke in swimming?

a) *Daley Thompson* b) *Jesse Owens*
c) *Carl Lewis* d) *Victor Davis*

138. Daley Thompson apparently missed a new world record in winning his second consecutive gold medal in the decathlon; the next year his score was retroactively raised to . . . giving him the record.

a) *8457* b) *8677*
c) *8787* d) *8847*

139. Mary Lou Retton became the first ... outside Eastern Europe to win the all-around competition.

a) *Gymnast* b) *Cyclist*
c) *Swimmer* d) *Rider*

140. Steve Redgrave won his first title in ... of the record five he would go on to win in five Olympic competitions.

a) *Rowing* b) *Equestrian*
c) *Swimming* d) *Athletics*

1988 Olympics

141. Who won four gold medals in gymnastics?

a) *Daniela Silivas* b) *Roy Jones Jr.*
c) *Vladimir Artemov* d) *Lawrence Lemieux*

142. Florence Griffith Joyner won three gold medals and a silver on the track. Which country did she represent?

a) *USA* b) *Canada*
c) *UK* d) *Australia*

143. Lawrence Lemieux, a ... sailor in the Finn class, was in second place and poised to win a silver medal when he abandoned the race to save an injured competitor. He arrived in 21st place, but was recognised by the IOC with a special award honouring his bravery and sacrifice.

a) *USA* b) *British*
c) *Kiwi* d) *Canadian*

144. Who became the first (and last) athlete to win Olympic medals at the Winter Olympics and Summer Olympics in the same year. She added a cycling silver to the speed skating gold she won earlier in the Winter Olympics of that year in Calgary?

a) *Kerstin Palm*
b) *Christa Luding-Rothenburger*
c) *Florence Griffith Joyner*
d) *Evelyn Ashford*

145. Name the player who won his second consecutive individual gold medal in the three-day event in equestrian on Charisma,

only the second time in history that a gold medal had been won consecutively.

a) *Mark Todd* b) *Greg Louganis*
c) *Vladimir Artemov* d) *Daniela Silivas*

1992 Olympics

146. In gymnastics, who won six gold medals, including four on a single day?

a) *Vitaly Scherbo* b) *Eric Heiden*
c) *Fu Mingxia* d) *Chris Boardman*

147. Evelyn Ashford won her ... Olympic gold medal in the 4x100 metre relay, making her one of only four female athletes to have achieved this in history.

a) *Sixth* b) *Fifth*
c) *Fourth* d) *Third*

148. On the 20th anniversary of the Munich massacre, ... Yael Arad became the first to win an Olympic medal, winning a silver medal in judo.

a) *Israeli* b) *Ethiopian*
c) *Arab* d) *Indonesian*

149. Who won the 100 m at the age of 32?

a) *Florence Griffith Joyner* b) *Linford Christie*
c) *Evelyn Ashford* d) *Kerstin Palm*

150. ... swimmers dominated the freestyle events, with Alexander Popov and Yevgeny Sadovyi both winning two events.

a) *Russian* b) *Vitaly Scherbo*
c) *Eric Heiden* d) *Fu Mingxia*

1996 Olympics

151. Who won the badminton men's singles in Atlanta?

a) *Rexy Mainaky* b) *Rashid Sid[illegible]*
c) *Jiong Dong* d) *Poul-Erik H[illegible]er-Larsen*

152. **Who were the first winners of Olympic gold in men's beach volleyball at Atlanta and defenders of that title in Sydney?**

a) *Mike Dodd and Mike Whitmarsh*

b) *Kach Kiraly and Kent Steffes*

c) *John Child and Mark Heese*

d) *Andrea Zorzi and Silvio Bettega*

153. **Who was the winner in gymnastics artistic women's individual?**

a) *Shannon Miller* b) *Lilia Podkopayeva*

c) *Gina Gogean* d) *Simona Amanar*

154. **Who won the gold medal on the cycling road-event?**

a) *Miguel Indurain* b) *Max Sciandri*

c) *Rolf Sorensen* d) *Pascal Richard*

155. **In judo, who was the men's champion heavyweight 95+ in Atlanta?**

a) *David Douillet* b) *Harry van Barneveld*

c) *Ernesto Perez* d) *Frank Moller*

2000 Olympics

156. **Australia won its 100th Olympic Gold Medal during the 2000 games. Which athlete was the proud recipient of the medal?**

a) *Merlene Ottey* b) *Ian Thorpe*

c) *Cathy Freeman* d) *Susie O'Neill*

157. **Nova Peris-Kneebone is now a runner but she has won Olympic gold in another sport. What is that sport?**

a) *Hockey* b) *Tennis*

c) *Swimming* d) *Softball*

158. **Who won the men's individual final in archery?**

a) *Victor Wanderle* b) *Simon Fairweather*

c) *Wietse van Atkin* d) *Jared Larsen*

159. Who won the men's hammer throw?

a) *Ivan Tikhon (Belarus)*
b) *Nicola Vizzoni (Italy)*
c) *Szyman Ziolkowski (Poland)*
d) *Igor Astapkovich (Belarus)*

160. Who won the women's 100 m sprint?

a) *Merlene Ottey (Jamacia)*
b) *Ekaterini Thanou (Greece)*
c) *Marion Jones (USA)*
d) *Tanya Lawrence (Jamacia)*

161. Who won the men's discus throw?

a) *Lars Riedel (Germany)*
b) *Virgilijus Alenka (Lithuania)*
c) *Frantz Kruger (South Africa)*
d) *Vasily Kaptyukh (Belarus)*

162. Who won the men's javelin throw?

a) *Jan Zelezny (Czech Republic)*
b) *Sergey Makarov (Russia)*
c) *Steve Backley (Great Britain)*
d) *Raymond Hecht (Germany)*

163. Who won the women's heptathlon?

a) *Denise Lewis (Great Britain)*
b) *Natalya Sazanovich (Belarus)*
c) *Yelena Prokhorova (Russia)*
d) *Urszula Wlodarczyk (Poland)*

164. Who won the women's pole vault?

a) *Stacy Dragila (USA)*
b) *Vala Flosadottir (Iceland)*
c) *Tatiana Grigorieva (Australia)*
d) *Daniela Bartova (Czech Republic)*

165. Who won the Women's 20 km Walk?

a) *Kjersti Plaetzer (Norway)*
b) *Wang Liping (China)*
c) *Maria Vasco (Spain)*
d) *Erica Alfridi (Italy)*

166. In cycling, men's one km time trial, the gold medal was won by Jason Queally from Britain. But who won the silver medal?

a) *Chris Boardman - United Kingdom*
b) *Shane Kelly - Australia*
c) *Stefan Nimke – Germany*
d) *Erik Dekker - The Netherlands*

167. In judo, women's extra lightweight, who lost the final and won the silver medal?

a) *Ryoko Tamura - Japan*
b) *Ann Simons - Belgium*
c) *Lioubov Brouletova – Russia*
d) *Anna-Maria Gradante – Germany*

168. In shooting, women's air rifle, who won the gold medal?

a) *Nancy Johnson - United States*
b) *Cho-Hyun Kang - Korea*
c) *Pia Hansen - Sweden*
d) *Jong Gao - China*

169. In canoe-kayak, men's C-1 slalom, who won the gold medal?

a) *Juraj Mincik - Slovakia*
b) *Michal Martikan - Slovakia*
c) *Tony Estanguet - France*
d) *Ed Moses - United States*

170. In swimming, women's 100 m backstroke, who won the gold medal?

a) *Leisel Jones - Australia*
b) *Diana Mocanu - Romania*
c) *Nina Zhivanevskaya - Spain*
d) *Mai Nakamura – Japan*

171. In shooting, women's air pistol, the gold medal was won by whom?

a) *Nancy Johnson - United States*
b) *Jasna Sekaric - Yugoslavia*
c) *Annemarie Forder - Australia*
d) *Luna Tao - China*

172. In cycling, women's 500 m time trial, who won the gold medal?

a) *Leontien Zijlaard-Van Moorsel - The Netherlands*
b) *Michelle Ferris - Australia*
c) *Felicia Ballanger - France*
d) *Cuihua Jiang - China*

173. Who won the women's long jump?

a) *Fiona May (Italy)*
b) *Tatiana Kotova (Russia)*
c) *Marion Jones (USA)*
d) *Heike Drechsler (Germany)*

174. Who won the men's decathalon?

a) *Roman Serble (Czech Republic)*
b) *Erki Nool (Estonia)*
c) *Chris Huffins (USA)*
d) *Dean Macey (Great Britain)*

175. Who won the men's high jump?

a) *Sergey Kluigin (Russia)*
b) *Abderrahmane Hammad (Algeria)*
c) *Javier Sotomayer (Cuba)*
d) *Stefan Holm (Sweden)*

2004 Olympics

176. Who was the famous American swimmer who won five gold medals?

a) *Michael Phelps*
b) *Ryan Lochte*
c) *Aaron Peirsol*
d) *Ian Crocker*

177. Which female gymnast won the gold medal in the women's all around final?

a) *Zhang Nan (CHN)* b) *Svetlana Khorkina (RUS)*
c) *Carly Patterson (US)* d) *Anna Pavlova (RUS)*

178. In which race did G-ry Hall win the gold swimming?

a) *50 m freestyle* b) *100 m butterfly*
c) *100 m freestyle* d) *50 m butterfly*

179. Which two athletes secured historic track doubles, by winning both events they competed in?

a) *Jeremy Wariner & Veronica Campbell*
b) *Kelly Holmes & Hicham El Guerrouj*
c) *Justin Gatlin & Tonique Williams-Darling*
d) *Dwight Phillips & Yumiliedi Cumba*

180. The winner of the 50 metre freestyle is classified as the world's fastest swimmer. Who won this event in the women's division?

a) *Malia Metella* b) *Jenny Thompson*
c) *Kara Lynn Joyce* d) *Inge de Bruijn*

181. Who won the men's 200 metre backstroke?

a) *Aaron Peirsol* b) *Razvan Florea*
c) *Markus Rogan* d) *James Goddard*

182. Kostas Kenteris, the Greek sprinter, injured in a motorcycle crash and the centre of drug allegations, won the gold medal in which event in the Sydney Olympics?

a) *200 m* b) *400 m* c) *100 m* d) *800 m*

183. Ireland won one medal, and that was gold in the form of Cian O'Connor, but in which sport?

a) *Road walking* b) *Decathlon*
c) *Trap shooting* d) *Equestrian*

184. Who won the men's 200 metre freestyle event?

a) *Pieter van den Hoogenband* b) *Michael Phelps*
c) *Ian Thorpe* d) *Klete Keller*

185. Which Australian shooter, going for his third consecutive gold medal, missed the final of the men's trap?

a) *Roy Slaven* b) *Adam Vella*
c) *Michael Diamond* d) *Russel Mark*

186. Kirsty Coventry won the first swimming gold medal for Zimbabwe in what event?

a) *200 m individual medley* b) *100 m backstroke*
c) *400 m individual medley* d) *200 m backstroke*

187. In the women's beach volleyball final, Americans Misty May and Kerri Walsh faced a team from where?

a) *Spain* b) *England*
c) *Brazil* d) *China*

188. An American runner won the gold, silver, and bronze, in all but which of the following races?

a) *The men's 200 m*
b) *An American won each colour of medal in all these races*
c) *The men's 400 m* d) *The men's 100 m*

189. Rulon Gardiner, who won the gold, is which kind of wrestler?

a) *Greco-Roman* b) *Professional*
c) *Freestyle* d) *Sumo*

190. American Laura Wilkinson participated in which type of diving?

a) *3 m springboard* b) *10 m platform*
c) *10 m synchronised platform*
d) *3 m synchronised platform*

191. How many silver medals did Great Britain and Germany secure combined?

a) *25* b) *35* c) *30* d) *40*

192. In boxing, how many gold medals were won by the Cuban boxers?

a) *4* b) *2* c) *3* d) *5*

193. Paul Hamm won the men's all-around final. What was his placement after four rotations?

a) *10* b) *12* c) *8* d) *6*

194. Not including the all-around men's medal, how many individual medals did Paul Hamm win?

a) *3* b) *0* c) *1* d) *2*

195. Which member of the American woman's 4 x 200 metre freestyle relay was the youngest?

a) *Natalie Coughlin* b) *Dana Vollmer*
c) *Amanda Beard* d) *Kaitlin Sandeno*

196. Which of the following is not true?

a) *The US men's basketball team had the wrong jerseys, delaying the bronze medal match.*

b) *American swimmer Aaron Piersol was disqualified in a race, costing him a gold medal.*

c) *The women's soccer gold medal match was delayed while a referee was being replaced.*

d) *A marathon runner was jumped by a bystander.*

197. How many times did Michael Phelps race Ian Thorpe in an individual (not team relay) finals race?

a) *Twice* b) *Four times*
c) *Three times* d) *Once*

198. Who did Michael Phelps give up his spot for in the last swim meet?

a) *Jason Lezak* b) *Aaron Piersol*
c) *Ian Crocker* d) *Brendan Hanson*

199. Michael Phelps won his first gold medal of the Olympics in which event?

a) *200 m individual medley* b) *400 m individual medley*
c) *200 m butterfly* d) *200 m freestyle*

200. US gymnast Brett McClure was engaged to marry what other famous gymnast?

a) *Amanda Borden* b) *Kristen Maloney*
c) *Jamie Dantzscher* d) *Jaycie Phelps*

Answers

Ancient Games

1. 776 BC
2. Pausanias
3. The ancient Greeks
4. Zeus
5. The ivory, gold-adorned statue of Zeus (sculpted by the legendary Phidias)
6. A running race
7. Ekecheiria
8. 200 yard footrace
9. Nothing
10. Wıeath of olives branches
11. 10 months
12. Their city-states
13. Train faithfully for ten months before the games, remain under the eyes of officials for a month, and take an oath that they had fulfilled the training requirements.
14. Chariot racing
15. She could be thrown off a cliff.

16. All of the above

17. Leonidas of Rhodes

18. 200 metres

19. A town north of Athens where the Athenians defeated the invading Persians

20. Nero

21. Jason (of the Argonauts fame)

22. 400 yards

23. Plato

24. 708 BC

25. Nero

26. AD 393

27. 688 BC

28. An ancient Greek unit of time

29. Hippodrome

30. A mounted archery tournament

31. Greek

32. AD 393

33. Coroebus

34. Olympia

35. Theodosius

Modern Games

1. Athens, Greece

2. 1896

3. 9

4. 245
5. Greece
6. Commercialism in sports
7. The triple jump
8. Badminton
9. Olympia, Greece
10. Paris
11. 19
12. Broken telephone poles
13. Women's events were cut back.
14. Women were allowed to compete.
15. 22
16. Boxing
17. Pole vault
18. Boxing
19. Barcelona
20. Amsterdam 1928
21. 1936
22. 1928
23. A gymnastics manoeuvre
24. 1960s
25. USA
26. Australia
27. Stefan Holm
28. Three times

29. Millennium

30. Speed skating

31. Five days

32. Alone in a cemetery

33. USA

34. 1976

35. Rajyavardhan S. Rathore

36. Jesse Owens

37. Australia, France, Great Britain, Greece and Switzerland

38. Athens, Greece

39. Munich

40. He wore no shoes in his first of two marathons.

41. Beach volleyball

42. 800 m and 1500 m

43. Justin Gatlin

44. Weightlifting

45. Trampoline tumbling

46. Melbourne 1956

47. Athena and Phevos – a brother and sister named after Greek gods

48. Yulia Nesterenko

49. Pieter Van den Hoggenband

50. Settled in North America

51. Yuriy Bilonog

52. USA

53. Carl Lewis

54. India

55. Xiang Liu

56. 100 metres

67. Ian Thorpe

58. Two years

59. 1924

60. 398

61. 13

62. St Louis

63. Australia

64. Stockholm

65. Pentathlon and Decathlon

66. HRH Prince Hendrik

67. Javelin and 80 metre hurdles

68. USA

69. November

70. 10.25

71. Chris Rinke

72. Bart Brentjens

73. Nova Perris Kneebone

74. Athens, Greece

75. London

76. Great Britain

77. 10 hours 42 minutes

78. Germany

79. India

80. Alfred Oerter Jr

81. 0

82. USA

83. Justin Huish

84. SOBO

85. Nikki Webster

86. Wheelchair racing

87. No country boycotted the Olympics

88. Phevos and Athena

89. Shooting

90. Great Britain

91. 5

92. Uruguay

93. Japan

94. 33 events, 24 for men and 9 for women

95. Alain Mimoun

96. Ennio Falco

97. Bondi Beach

98. USA

99. Canada in 1976

100. Eight

101. John Hayes (USA)

102. Hawaiian

193. 100 metres freestyle swimming

104. 19

105. 16

106. Rechelle Hawkes

107. Grant Hackett

108. Austria

109. Betty Cuthbert

110. In the closing ceremony athletes did not walk in team formation.

111. Amsterdam 1928

112. Five days

113. Munich

114. Australia

115. Croatia

116. Alone in a cemetery

117. 312

118. Weightlifting

119. Soo-Hyun Bang

120. Netherlands

History and Trivia

1. 200 yard, 400 yard foot race and a variable length foot race

2. 1912 in Stockholm

3. Cook

4. Marathon

5. Peloponnesian

6. Tug-of-war

7. 1968, Mexico City

8. French

9. French

10. Los Angeles

11. The most important thing in the Olympic games is not to win, but to take part.

12. Australia

13. London

14. Berlin, Tokyo and Helsinki

15. 1,500

16. Boxing and wrestling

17. 1924

18. Lausanne

19. Brown

20. Pentathletes

21. A man should spend his whole life at play.

22. Ball games, which were often played with pig's bladders or, even earlier that that, skulls.

23. She was the first person to get perfect 10s from all of the judges.

24. Enforced suicide - if the target was frequently missed, then suicide had to be carried out by the person who missed the target.

25. 1936 - Berlin

26. 1908 - London

27. 1976, 1980 and 1984

28. Altis

29. Horse Racing

30. Televising of the Games

31. Antwerp

32. All of these three answers are correct. The Egyptians left a lot of evidence for their love of sports.

33. 1908

34. A boulder or stone, weighing 350lb (159kg), being lifted to chest height.

35. Athens

36. 1982

37. A truce

38. Zeus

39. 1916, 1940 and 1944

40. Citius, Altius, Fortius

41. Amsterdam

42. Fencer

43. The games were held from 1800 BC until around AD 1180, and they were called The Tailteann Games.

44. 1920

45. 1928

46. Gymnasium

47. 1900 - Paris

48. Melbourne

49. Theodosius I

50. 1924

Olympic Facts

1. Baron Pierre de Coubertin
2. Cross-country running, swimming, pistol shooting, fencing and horseback riding
3. Germany
4. Roller hockey
5. Henry Didon
6. Swifter, Higher, Stronger
7. 2
8. The union of the five continents: America, Africa, Australia, Europe and Asia
9. 1936
10. 1948 London
11. Pierre de Coubertin
12. Fishing
13. Softball
14. Once in four years
15. Greeks
16. 2
17. 1961
18. Temple of Hera
19. Physically disabled
20. Scotland
21. Belgium
22. Japan in 1964
23. Greek

24. 26 miles

25. 1968 Mexico City

26. 1912

27. 1912 Stockholm

28. Rome in 1960

29. Sabre

30. 0-10

31. 6

32. Spyros Samaras

33. 1936 Berlin

34. English and French

35. 1908

36. Nenikekamen!

37. 1960

38. 1924

39. Los Angeles, 1932

40. Eva Klobukowska

41. Aladar Gerevich

42. 1896, Athens

43. 1904

44. Oscar Swahn

45. The ivory, gold-adorned statue of Zeus sculpted by the legendary Phidias

46. 26 miles 385 yards

47. Swimming

48. 52

49. Netherlands

50. Italy

51. Rome

52. September 5, 1997

53. They are the only Australians to win three gold medals in the same event at three different Olympics.

54. Reining

55. Mohini Bhardwaj and the floor exercise

56. Paris

57. 24

58. World's Fair

59. Cups or trophies

60. Two-day cricket

61. Children

62. USA

63. 13

64. Croquet

65. France

66. Equestrian

67. French

68. America's

69. Polo

70. River Seine

71. France

72. 26
73. Charlotte Cooper
74. David Francis
75. 6
76. Decathlon
77. Basketball
78. USA
79. Finnish
80. Swedish
81. American
82. Italy
83. Pennsylvania
84. Frederick
85. 22
86. Rings
87. Swimming and diving
88. General George S. Patton
89. Electronic timing devices
90. Serbia
91. Antwerp
92. Turkey
93. Doves
94. Ice hockey
95. Faster, Higher, Stronger
96. Ireland

97. Uruguay
98. Amsterdam
99. Prince Hendrik
100. Greece
101. Gymnastics
102. India
103. Coca-Cola
104. Germany
105. India
106. Norway
107. Victory podium
108. Boulevard
109. American football and lacrosse
110. Republic of China
111. 49
112. Olympia
113. Aryan race
114. Olympia
115. Seventy hours
116. Basketball and handball
117. The Republic of China's
118. Canada
119. Sweden
120. Finland
121. Diplomas

122.Sprint athletics

123.Empire Stadium

124.Paavo Nurmi and Hannes Kolehmainen

125.Hungary

126.Gold

127.Melbourne

128.Philip, Duke of Edinburgh

129.USA's

130.Melbourne

131.Iraq

132.Switzerland

133.Formosa

134.Olympia

135.Ron Clarke

136.Australian

137.Switzerland

138.Russia

139.Lake Wendouree

140.Port Phillip Bay

141.Soviet

142.1992

143.1912

144.Pakistan

145.Flaminio Stadium

146.Tokyo

147.USA

148.Yuji Koseki

149.Yoshinori Sakai

150.Baseball and judo

151.Sixteen

152.Nippon Budokan

153.112

154.For life

155.Norma Enriqueta Basilio

156.National Auditorium

157.Munich

158.Heidi Schüller

159.18

160.1936

161.1920

162.Referees

163.Badminton and water skiing

164.Waldi, the dachshund

165.13

166.Mark Spitz

167.Maurice Fauget

168.The host country

169.Congo's

170.Olympic Stadium

171.Ottawa

172.9.7

173.80

174.USA

175.15

176.21

177.Central Lenin Stadium

178.Zimbabwe

179.8th

180.East Germany

181.Hungary

182.Misha, the bear cub

183.Men's Triple Jump

184.East German

185.He ran only in the 10,000 metres.

186.Libya

187.Brazilian

188.Morocco

189.Tennis

190.Dancer

191.Los Angeles Memorial Coliseum

192.Seoul, South Korea

193.Lee Hakrae

194.Suriname

195.China

196.Barcelona

197.Men

198.28

199.Arrow

200.64

201.Cuba

202.Afghanistan

203.French

204.Dog Cobi

205.Netherlands

206.USA

207.USA

208.Rachelle Hawkes

209.3

210.Tina Arena

211.Hockey

212.Hidden Creek's Perin

213.Korea

214.Switzerland

215.Brazil

216.Germany

217.Italy

218.China

219.USA

220.Cuba

221.Andrew Gaze

222.Homebush Bay

223.Turkey

224.USA

225.Cuba

226.Football

227.Russia

228.France

229.4

230.USA

231.USA

232.Kiribati and Timor-Leste

233.16

234.115-115

235.A racer stumbled over one of the hurdles.

236.The high bar event

237.2

238.USA

239.Bronze

240.Uneven bars

241.Romania

242.Romania & Germany

243.Germany & Australia

244.China

245.1908 Games in London

246.192.2 metres

247.Buenos Aires, Cape Town, Rome & Stockholm

248.The women's volleyball team

249.The US Open in tennis

250.Men's 200 m

251.New Zealand

252.Australia

253.August 13th to 29th.

254.Russia

255.Cuba

256.Bronze

257.Australia

258.Ukraine

259.The US baseball team

260.Argentina

Winter Olympics

1. Calgary 1988
2. 1924
3. Derek Parra
4. Chamonix-Mont-Blanc, France
5. 19th
6. 4
7. Bulgaria
8. Germany
9. Spain

10. A triple flip
11. February 10 - February 26
12. 8
13. Mountaineering
14. Kitty ears
15. Most countries are too warm to host the Winter Games.
16. Calgary, Canada
17. Vicks
18. The medal was awarded to a rival in error.
19. Mike Modano
20. Bonnie Blair
21. 2
22. Chamonix in France
23. Sonja Henie
24. Luge
25. Dorothy Hamill
26. Torino, Italy
27. Snowboard cross
28. A high-speed, face-down, head-first sledding event
29. Bobsleigh
30. A female snowball and a male ice cube
31. Apolo Anton Ohno
32. Jack Hughes
33. Belgium
34. Figure skating

45. Ski jumping

46. Vancouver, Canada

37. Played them the Japanese anthem at the hardest part of the course.

38. Ross Powers

39. Canada

40. Curling

41. Germany

42. Patrol race

43. Michelle Kwan

44. John Furlong and Jack Poole

45. Curling

46. Norway

47. Awesome Dawson

48. Canada

49. Buzz Schneider

50. Ukraine

51. 10

52. Switzerland

53. Broke the world record in three different events.

54. Herbies

55. Australia

56. Germany

57. The original dance

58. 4th

59. First growing place of the distinctive uva blu wine

60. Lindsey Jacobellis
61. Cross-country skiing and shooting
62. Tara Lipinski
63. Bruce Horsch
64. Great Britain
65. Great Britain
66. 12
67. Vladimir Krutov
68. Norway
69. Canada
70. USA
71. Prince Albert of Monaco
72. Australia and Spain
73. Ole Einar Bjoerndalen (Norway)
74. Turkey
75. Ice Cube

Winners and Medals

1. Spiridon Louis
2. Carl Schuhmann
3. Thomas Burke
4. Paul Masson
5. Adolf Schmal
6. Aristidis Konstantinidis
7. Leonidas Pyrgos
8. Eugène-Henri Gravelotte
9. Hermann Weingärtner
10. Alfred Flatow

11. Carl Schuhmann
12. Pantelis Karasevdas
13. Alfréd Hajós
14. Germany
15. Friedrich Traun
16. Alvin Kraenzlein
17. Charlotte Cooper
18. Twenty
19. Italian
20. Switzerland's
21. Four
22. Canada's
23. Discus thrower
24. American
25. Swimming
26. Six
27. Steeplechase
28. Harry Hillman
29. Ralph Rose
30. 28
31. Ray Ewry
32. 72
33. Pavao
34. England
35. Porter

36. Jim Thorpe
37. Deer-shooting
38. Great Britain
39. Finland
40. 100 m
41. Five
42. Finland
43. 1500
44. Ville Ritola
45. Finnish
46. 100
47. Eric Liddell
48. Douglas Lowe
49. Water polo
50. France
51. Albert Seguin
52. Mikio Oda of Japan
53. 10,000 metres
54. 100 and 200 metres
55. 100 and 200 metres
56. Babe Didrikson
57. 1980
58. A professional
59. Swimming
60. Press reporter

61. 100
62. Four
63. The Netherlands
64. Fifth
65. German
66. Dutch
67. William Porter
68. Decathlon
69. Roy Cochran
70. Ceylon
71. Denmark
72. Marathon
73. 7,887
74. Vladimir Kuts
75. This event wasn't run until 1972.
76. Adhemar da Silva (BRA)
77. 1. BJ Morrow USA 2. A. Stanfield USA 3. T. Baker USA
78. Sydney
79. Australian
80. Pat McCormick
81. Great Britain's
82. Ron Delaney
83. Chris Brasher
84. 9 1/4
85. Norway

86. Fourth
87. Greece
88. Hungary
89. Polio
90. 25 km
91. Cassius Clay
92. Canoer
93. 1500
94. Decathlon
95. Swimming
96. Dutchman
97. 189-0
98. 18
99. Australian
100. 9.9
101. Second
102. George Foreman
103. Czechoslovakia
104. Debbie Meyer
105. 8.90
106. Mark Spitz
107. Olga Korbut
108. Finland
109. Valeri Borzov
110. Life

111. Romania
112. USSR
113. Italy
114. Cuba
115. Davis
116. Coe, Straub, Ovett, Busse
117. Anatoli Bondarchuk
118. Linda Haglund
119. Tomi Poikolainen
120. Ketevan Losaberidze
121. Cuban
122. Tatiana Kazankina
123. Lutz Dombrowski
124. Great Britain
125. Teófilo Stevenson
126. Cycling
127. Martina Jaschke
128. Petre Rosca
129. Roland Bruckner
130. Soviet
131. Hans Kjeld Rasmussen
132. Vladimir Salnikov
133. Yurik Vardanyan
134. Wrestling
135. Sergei Kornilaev

136. Long Jump

137. Victor Davis

138. 8847

139. Gymnast

140. Rowing

141. Vladimir Artemov

142. USA

143. Canadian

144. Christa Luding-Rothenburger

145. Mark Todd

146. Vitaly Scherbo

147. Fourth

148. Israeli

149. Linford Christie

150. Russian

151. Poul-Erik Hoyer-Larsen

152. Kach Kiraly and Kent Steffes

153. Lilia Podkopayeva

154. Pascal Richard

155. David Douillet

156. Cathy Freeman

157. Hockey

158. Simon Fairweather

159. Szyman Ziolkowski

160. Marion Jones

161. Virgilijus Alenka

162. Jan Zelezny

163. Denise Lewis

164. Stacy Dragila

165. Wang Liping

166. Stefan Nimke

167. Lioubov Brouletova

168. Nancy Johnson

169. Juraj Mincik

170. Diana Mocanu

171. Luna Tao - China

172. Felicia Ballanger

173. Heike Drechsler

174. Erki Nool

175. Sergey Kluigin

176. Michael Phelps

177. Carly Patterson

178. 50 m freestyle

179. Kelly Holmes & Hicham El Guerrouj

180. Inge de Bruijn

181. Aaron Peirsol

182. 200 m

183. Equestrian

184. Ian Thorpe

185. Michael Diamond

186. 200 m backstroke

187. Brazil

188. The men's 100 m

189. Greco-Roman

190. 10 m platform

191. 25

192. 5

193. 12

194. 1

195. Dana Vollmer

196. American swimmer Aaron Piersol was disqualified in a race, costing him a gold medal.

197. Once

198. Ian Crocker

199. 400 m individual medley

200. Jaycie Phelps